THE
I USED TO
KNOW THAT
ACTIVITY BOOK

THE
I USED TO KNOW THAT
ACTIVITY BOOK

STUFF YOU FORGOT FROM SCHOOL

CAROLINE TAGGART

Michael O'Mara Books Limited

*Very many thanks to Oli Dacombe, who drafted the maths
and science chapters with enthusiasm, imagination and
more accuracy than I could have managed.*

This new edition first published in 2016

First published in Great Britain in 2012 by
Michael O'Mara Books Limited
9 Lion Yard
Tremadoc Road
London SW4 7NQ

A CIP catalogue record for this book is available from the British Library.

Papers used by Michael O'Mara Books Limited are natural, recyclable products
made from wood grown in sustainable forests. The manufacturing processes
conform to the environmental regulations of the country of origin.

ISBN: 978-1-78243-661-4

1 2 3 4 5 6 7 8 9 10

www.mombooks.com

Designed and typeset by www.glensaville.com

Printed and bound by CPI Group (UK) Ltd, Croydon, CR0 4YY

CONTENTS

INTRODUCTION

The point of the original book *I Used to Know That* was to remind us all of things that we had once known and that were lingering somewhere in the back of our minds. Because it didn't deal with anything beyond O-level/GCSE standard, it inevitably covered subjects that were part of a compulsory curriculum, the ones we had to take whether we liked it or not. It included formulae and dates we learnt without understanding or caring why; names and places that we would never think of again once the exams were over. But it was supposed to be fun, nostalgic, even informative – it certainly didn't set out to stir up bad memories.

And yet . . . And yet . . . When I talked to people about *I Used to Know That*, it was always the horror stories they wanted to recall. Spelling tests, punctuation problems and remind me again what a hypotenuse is: it was that sort of thing that touched a chord.

So, when we came to put this book together, we didn't flinch. Yes, there are some things just for fun – trivia, if you like, or knowledge for knowledge's sake. But most of it is stuff that you probably learnt at school and that you do have hidden away somewhere in the back of those dusty mental filing cabinets. Pythagoras is in here; so are adjectives and adverbs; *Wuthering Heights* and *Tess of the D'Urbervilles*; the difference between an atoll and an archipelago, a vein and an artery; and the half-life of plutonium (whatever that means).

Are you feeling nervous? It gets worse.

We have called this an 'activity' book. Who are we trying to kid? Almost everything here takes the form of a quiz (if you want to take it playfully) or a test (if you see the whole thing as something darker and more menacing). How you tackle them is entirely up to you. Complete them by yourself or in competition with someone else. Do them against the clock or in your own time. Award marks or not, just as you like. But whatever approach you take, remember this: there'll be some ghostly invigilatory presence there, looking over your shoulder, pointing out where you've gone wrong, muttering words like 'pass', 'fail', and possibly 'stupid boy'.

You wanted painful memories? Here they are. I hope you enjoy them.

CAROLINE TAGGART

1 ENGLISH LANGUAGE

It's what we speak and write every day of our lives, but how well do we do it? Do we really understand the words we use, or how to put them together accurately and effectively? Have a go at these tests and see just how competent you are in your mother tongue.

1 Parts of Speech

Purists argue about what exactly constitutes a 'part of speech' and therefore how many of them there are, but let's no go there: let's say there are nine. These are noun, pronoun, adjective, verb, adverb, preposition, conjunction, determiner and interjection. They are the building blocks of a sentence and each performs a separate function. As I am sure you know – or used to know.

So rather than patronize you by telling you that a noun is a naming word and a verb is a doing word, let's try you out on a few sample sentences. Underline, circle, highlight or just shout out the nouns, pronouns and adjectives in the following:

1. In my younger and more vulnerable years my father gave me some advice.
2. The scene was a plain, bare, monotonous vault of a schoolroom.
3. At Paris, just after dark one gusty evening, I was enjoying the twofold luxury of a meditation and a meerschaum.

2 Parts of Speech 2

Now let's try verbs, adverbs and prepositions – and remember that it's possible for a verb to be made up of more than one word.

1. It is a far, far better thing that I do, than I have ever done.
2. All emotions, and that one particularly, were abhorrent to his cold, precise, but admirably balanced mind.
3. The family of Dashwood had been long settled in Sussex.

3 Parts of Speech 3

Finally, spot the conjunctions, determiners and interjections in this extract:

'Ahem!' said Mr Micawber, clearing his throat, and warming with the punch and with the fire. 'My dear, another glass?'

Mrs Micawber said it must be very little; but we couldn't allow that, so it was a glassful.

Answers on page 151–2

4 Keep It Simple

One of the first rules of good writing is never to use a big word when a little one will do. A rule, of course, that is made to be broken, because some of the big words are irresistible. But it's worth bearing in mind, so that if someone accuses you of being pretentious, you can at least claim to be being pretentious on purpose.

Whatever your motives, can you match the fancy word in the upper list to the everyday alternatives in the lower?

1. Desipient
2. Effulgent
3. Inchoate
4. Lachrymose
5. Lubricious
6. Meretricious
7. Minutious
8. Nugatory
9. Otiose
10. Piligerous

A. Foolish
B. Hairy
C. Lewd
D. Nit-picking
E. Prone to weeping
F. Rudimentary, immature
G. Shining brightly
H. Superficially attractive, insincere
I. Trifling, of little importance
J. Useless, serving no purpose

Answers on page 152

5 Keep It Simple 2

You'll have noticed (I hope) that all the words in the previous quiz were adjectives, perhaps because it is in descriptions that we show the greatest tendency to go over the top. But try the same exercise with these verbs:

1. Bedizen
2. Beshrew
3. Confabulate
4. Contrist
5. Eructate
6. Lucubrate
7. Masticate
8. Obnubilate
9. Periclitate
10. Tergiversate

A. Burp
B. Chat or confer with
C. Chew
D. Darken, obscure
E. Decorate in a gaudy way
F. Endanger
G. Explain or amplify in a scholarly way
H. Forsake, abandon
I. Sadden
J. Wish harm on, curse

Answers on page 153

6 Get it Right

The problem with using those fancy words is that you run the risk of getting them wrong. The words in bold are all commonly misused; can you spot the mistakes in the following sentences and put them right? Be careful, though: some of the words are used correctly.

1. That scarf **complements** her dress beautifully.
2. I am completely **disinterested** in reality TV – I would far rather watch a good drama.
3. He's a very **egregious** person – he just loves going to parties.
4. She hadn't expected to marry for money, but she couldn't resist the **enormity** of his fortune.
5. I'm a hopeless swimmer: I tend to **flounder** around in the shallow end.
6. It was **fortuitous** that I bumped into him; otherwise I wouldn't have been able to tell him the news.
7. Anna had an excellent school report: her English teacher in particular gave her **fulsome** praise.
8. Do you mean to **imply** that you don't like my mother?
9. I'm always very **loathe** to arrive early in case there is no one to talk to.
10. She has been living in **straightened** circumstances since she had that disastrous holiday in Reno.

Answers on page 153

7 Where Do They All Come From?

English is an extraordinary mish-mash of a language, borrowing words from all over the world. Can you link the words listed to their countries of origin (in one instance a subdivision of a country) outlined on the map?

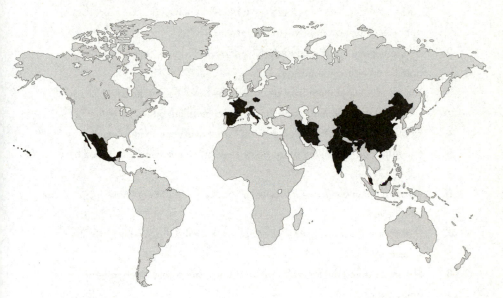

1. Algebra
2. Cenotaph
3. Chocolate
4. Compound
5. Diva
6. Macho
7. Robot
8. Shampoo
9. Typhoon
10. Ukulele

Answers on page 154

8 Which Is Which?

English is full of homophones and homonyms – words that sound or look the same but mean different things. In each of the following sentences, choose the correct word from the options given.

1. I didn't like to (*broach/brooch*) the subject of the missing (*broach/brooch*) because I knew Mother would be upset.

2. Before the election the candidate went out to (*canvas/canvass*) public opinion on education policy.

3. The head teacher (*censored/censured*) the boys' behaviour and (*censored/censured*) the rude magazine they were circulating to the rest of the class.

4. Please be (*discreet/discrete*): we don't want everyone to find out.

5. I must (*forego/forgo*) the pleasure of seeing you next week, as I shall be on holiday.

6. I wish to complain (*formally/formerly*) about the treatment I have been given.

7. There were (*hoards/hordes*) of people outside the shops waiting for the sales to start.

8. She hates going out for walks on cold days; she would much rather (*pore/pour*) over a book.

9. The (*principal/principle*) ran the school according to the simple (*principal/principle*) that whatever he said was law.

10. The horse was going too fast and she tried desperately to (*reign/rein*) it in.

9 Same Old, Same Old

In addition to homonyms, we also have synonyms and antonyms, words that mean, respectively, the same as each other or the opposite of each other. In this list, pair up the words with similar meanings.

1. Abreast
2. Acerbic
3. Amorphous
4. Benighted
5. Biting
6. Candid
7. Conversant
8. Desolate
9. Desultory
10. Devastated
11. Duplicitous
12. Formidable
13. Frank
14. Humane
15. Magnanimous
16. Ravaged
17. Redoubtable
18. Shapeless
19. Spasmodic
20. Wily

Answers on page 155.

10 Opposites Attract

In this test the words are antonyms – that is, they mean roughly the opposite of each other. Again, can you pair them up?

1. Assertive
2. Biased
3. Blatant
4. Congenial
5. Contemporary
6. Devious
7. Diaphanous
8. Dispassionate
9. Egotistical
10. Generous
11. Guileless
12. Lucid
13. Obscure
14. Obsequious
15. Obsolete
16. Opaque
17. Parsimonious
18. Repugnant
19. Selfless
20. Unobtrusive

Answers on page 155

11 Spelling

Are you any good at it? English is full of traps, confusions and illogicalities: sometimes you just have to learn a word or admit you don't know and look it up. The following list has ten words spelt correctly and ten incorrectly: can you sort them out and put the mistakes right?

1. Alledgedly
2. Appointed
3. Beseige
4. Calendar
5. Conferance
6. Connoisseur
7. Delicattessen
8. Deplorible
9. Extravagant
10. Fulfillment
11. Hygienic
12. Idiosyncracy
13. Innoculate
14. Mantlepiece
15. Merchandise
16. Negligible
17. Persevere
18. Rigourous
19. Tranquillity
20. Vacuum

Answers on page 156

12 Here Are the Answers; Now What's the Question?

Spelling is important, but so is a wide vocabulary. How good is yours? Can you supply the word from the definitions given? This time they are all nouns and, to help you out as I haven't given the answers, the definitions are listed in alphabetical order of the words they define.

1. Overbearing self-esteem or vanity; also a witty thought, particularly an over-fanciful one.

2. Confinement, particularly of a political prisoner or as a punishment for misbehaviour in school.

3. The art of effective speaking, with reference to clear pronunciation and voice production.

4. The act of freeing or the state of being freed, often used with reference to slaves or women.

5. Exceptional intellectual or creative power, something more than talent; a person endowed with such power.

6. A morbid anxiety about one's health; imagining oneself to be ill.

7. A fond, often sentimental remembrance of a past time.

8. A creature with a thick skin, such as an elephant or rhinoceros; hence an insensitive person.

9. A close, careful examination, particularly an official one looking for mistakes or evidence of corruption.

10. A tuft of threads or cords bound at one end and hanging loose at the other, used as an ornament on curtains or clothing.

Answers on page 156

13 A Question of Grammar

. . . or of syntax, punctuation or style. Each of the following sentences has something wrong with it. Can you put it right – and have a go at explaining what was wrong?

1.   I'll be able to send the paperwork to yourself by the end of the week.
2.   I don't want to go to work today, I'm going to phone in sick.
3.   We only drank one beer each: we weren't in the least bit drunk.
4.   Dancing with Michael, my skirt swirled around my ankles.
5.   You can either apologize right now or you can go to bed without any supper.
6.   I'm enclosing a donation from my husband and I.
7.   Can I ask you a favour?
8.   The guide who I spoke to didn't know what time the museum closed.
9.   Laura is the youngest of the two sisters.
10. Modern mathematics first originated in Ancient Egypt and Babylon.

14 Apostrophes? Who know's?

When it comes to punctuation, the apostrophe seems to cause more problems that everything else put together. I've left them out of the following sentences – can you put them back where they are needed, without falling into the trap of inserting them where they *aren't* needed?

1. I dont want you to use my car. Why cant you use yours?
2. Hers are the only children I like. Everyone elses babies look like stewed prunes.
3. Is that someones idea of a joke? I certainly dont think its funny.
4. The river rises in the mountains and flows very quickly for its first few miles.
5. The ladies cloakroom is upstairs; the mens is next to the porters lodge.
6. You can always recognize actresses, even the unknown ones: theirs are the voices you can hear across a crowded room.
7. The price of all shoes has been reduced in this weeks sale.
8. Well have to leave soon: its nearly midnight.
9. There are some very pretty girls clothes in the shops. Its much harder to buy presents for boys.
10. Everyones talking about the presidents promises.

Answers on page 158

15 Collective Nouns

A collective noun is one that is used to refer to a *collection* of individuals as if they were a single entity. Where people are concerned these can be sensible – *audience, jury, orchestra, team* – or silly, as in made-up expressions such as *a shower of meteorologists* or *a portfolio of stockbrokers*. Among the animal kingdom, however, there are a lot that could be described as traditional and which are rather more imaginative than *a herd of elephants*. Can you match creature to collective?

1.   Bevy
2.   Charm
3.   Intrusion
4.   Kindle
5.   Labour
6.   Murder
7.   Prickle
8.   Shiver
9.   Swarm
10. Tower

A.   Cockroaches
B.   Crows
C.   Giraffes
D.   Goldfinches
E.   Jellyfish
F.   Kittens
G.   Moles
H.   Partridges
I.   Porcupines
J.   Sharks

16 Why Do We Say . . . ?

A

B

C

D

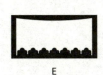

E

F

G

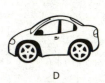

H

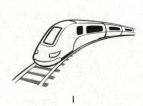

I

J

Answers on page 159

Match the cliché to the sport, form of transport or business (criminal business, in one case) from which it originated:

1. Firing on all cylinders
2. Hit the ground running
3. Safe pair of hands
4. Out of left field
5. Benchmark
6. Big picture
7. In the pipeline
8. A skeleton in the cupboard
9. To win hands down
10. To come up to scratch

Answers on page 159

17 Figures of Speech

Figures of speech are expressions in which words are used in a non-literal way or, more loosely, combined to produce a specific effect. Poets in particular love them. But can you match the technical terms to the examples?

1. Alliteration
2. Euphemism
3. Hyperbole
4. Litotes
5. Metaphor
6. Metonymy
7. Onomatopoeia
8. Oxymoron
9. Personification
10. Simile

A. a little local difficulty (as used by Prime Minister Harold Macmillan when three of his Treasury ministers resigned simultaneously)
B. a thousand thanks
C. all the world's a stage
D. as quick as lightning
E. bitter sweet
F. full fathom five my father lies
G. the murmuring of innumerable bees
H. Season of mists and mellow fruitfulness/Close bosom-friend of the maturing sun
I. to go the way of all flesh
J. Washington, meaning the US government

2 ENGLISH LITERATURE

Shakespeare, Dickens, the Brontës, Jane Austen and the rest — we've all been forced to read them at some time or another, and refreshed our memories with TV adaptations and films since. But how much do we really remember? Most of the answers in this chapter are given — it's just a matter of matching them up, so there's really no excuse. If you do badly, why not ask someone to give you a few boxed sets next birthday?

1 Classic Heroines

Match these young ladies to their nineteenth-century novels and supply the authors.

Clue: there are three by Jane Austen, three by Charles Dickens, two by different Brontës and two others.

1. Dorothea Brooke
2. Catherine Earnshaw
3. Anne Elliot
4. Lucie Manette
5. Catherine Morland
6. Fanny Price
7. Becky Sharp
8. Lucy Snowe
9. Esther Summerson
10. Agnes Wickfield

A. *Bleak House*
B. *David Copperfield*
C. *Mansfield Park*
D. *Middlemarch*
E. *Northanger Abbey*
F. *Persuasion*
G. *A Tale of Two Cities*
H. *Vanity Fair*
I. *Villette*
J. *Wuthering Heights*

Answers on page 161

2 More Recent 'Classics'

In the same spirit, match these twentieth-century characters to their novels and supply the authors.

1. Ralph, Jack and Piggy
2. Charles Arrowby
3. Pinkie Brown
4. Gudrun and Ursula Brangwen
5. Holden Caulfield
6. Jim Dixon
7. Scout and Jem Finch
8. Daphne Manners and Hari Kumar
9. George Milton and Lennie Small
10. Captain Yossarian and Major Major

A. *Brighton Rock*
B. *Catch-22*
C. *The Catcher in the Rye*
D. *The Jewel in the Crown*
E. *Lord of the Flies*
F. *Lucky Jim*
G. *Of Mice and Men*
H. *The Sea, the Sea*
I. *To Kill a Mockingbird*
J. *Women in Love*

Supplementary question: only one of the novelists won both the Man Booker Prize for Fiction (as it is now called) and the Nobel Prize in Literature. Who?

Clue: the first Booker Prize was awarded in 1969 and American authors are not eligible for it.

Answers on page 162

3 Pick a Colour

Fill in the gaps to form the titles of novels or short stories, and supply their authors. The missing words are all colours and the titles are listed in alphabetical order of those colours.

1. *The —— Spyglass*
2. *—— Beauty*
3. *The —— Cross (the first story to feature Father ——)*
4. *The —— Notebook*
5. *Anne of —— Gables*
6. *A Clockwork ——*
7. *The Color ——*
8. *The —— -Headed League*
9. *The —— Letter*
10. *—— Fang*

4 Pick a Number

In this quiz the missing words are all numbers. The one that is a complete blank is a novel published, contrary to what many people believe, in 1949. As an additional help, the answers are in numerical order, starting with the smallest. Of these ten works, one is a play, one is a collection of stories, the rest are novels.

1. A Tale of —— Cities
2. The —— Musketeers
3. The Sign of ——
4. —— Characters in Search of an Author
5. The —— —— Steps
6. Around the World in —— Days
7. —— —— Years of Solitude
8. The —— —— —— Dalmatians
9. The —— —— —— Nights
10. ——

Answers on page 162

5 Which Came First?

Starting with the earliest, list the following authors in the order of their birth.

1. Honoré de Balzac
2. Charlotte Brontë
3. Miguel de Cervantes
4. Anton Chekhov
5. Daniel Defoe
6. Johann von Goethe
7. Thomas Hardy
8. Henry Wadsworth Longfellow
9. Walt Whitman
10. Oscar Wilde

Answers on page 163

6 Which Came First 2:

Some More Recent Ones

Much more difficult, as they were all born within forty years of each other. If you're scoring, give yourself triple points for this one. If it helps, the earliest here is 1879 and the most recent 1919.

1. Samuel Beckett
2. Saul Bellow
3. F. Scott Fitzgerald
4. E. M. Forster
5. Doris Lessing
6. Vladimir Nabokov
7. George Orwell
8. Jean-Paul Sartre
9. Alexander Solzhenitsyn
10. J. R. R. Tolkien

Answers on page 163

7 Natural Features

Match the key words to the poets who wrote about them and give the name of the poem.

1. An albatross
2. Apes and peacocks
3. Daffodils
4. Fields of barley and of rye
5. Leaves of grass
6. A nightingale
7. A skylark
8. Thistles
9. A tyger
10. Willows and willowherb

A. William Blake
B. Samuel Taylor Coleridge
C. Ted Hughes
D. John Keats
E. John Masefield
F. Percy Bysshe Shelley
G. Alfred, Lord Tennyson
H. Edward Thomas
I. Walt Whitman
J. William Wordsworth

8 Potted Plots 1

This is one for those who are happy to impress their friends at dinner parties, rather than knowing anything in depth. Match the brief summaries to the book titles and the authors.

1. 'Okie' family leave the Dust Bowl for California during the 1930s Depression
2. Boy from a humble background is taken to London to be turned into a 'gentleman' on the wishes of an unknown benefactor
3. Miserly weaver adopts a little girl and learns to love something other than money
4. Girl from a humble background becomes the governess in the home of a wealthy man and hears strange noises coming from the attic
5. Soldier returning from World War I rents a house in Long Island, next to the mansion of a man renowned for his lavish parties
6. Young woman remains virtuous despite being abducted by her ruthless suitor – he is forced to drug and rape her in order to overcome her resistance
7. Poor country girl goes to work for a rich family with a similar surname to hers, with tragic consequences
8. Young man is abducted and forced to work as a cabin boy aboard a disreputable ship after discovering that he, not his miserly uncle, is heir to the family estate
9. The bored wife of a country doctor embarks on a series of affairs
10. The fortunes of a family of wealthy merchants decline over four generations

A. *Buddenbrooks*
B. *Clarissa*
C. *The Grapes of Wrath*
D. *Great Expectations*
E. *The Great Gatsby*
F. *Jane Eyre*
G. *Kidnapped*
H. *Madame Bovary*

Answers on page 164

I.   *Silas Marner*

J.   *Tess of the D'Urbervilles*

I.   Charlotte Brontë

II.   Charles Dickens

III.   George Eliot

IV.   F. Scott Fitzgerald

V.   Gustave Flaubert

VI.   Thomas Hardy

VII.   Thomas Mann

VIII. Samuel Richardson

IX.   John Steinbeck

X.   Robert Louis Stevenson

9 Potted Plots 2

OK, let's make it harder this time – you have to produce the titles and authors for yourself.

Hint: keep an open mind. Not all the books were written in English. Also, to help you, they are given in chronological order, with the earliest first.

1.   An elderly gentleman's head is turned by reading too many tales of chivalry. He decides he is a knight errant and sets out to have adventures.

2.   In a rambling comic autobiography, the hero isn't born until Volume IV.

3.   A young woman who has been reading too many Gothic novels nearly loses the man she loves because she imagines that his father has murdered his mother.

4.   A young woman pretends to be a widow to disguise the fact that she is separated from a drunken husband. Because this is a Victorian novel, the drunken husband dies, leaves her a fortune and enables her to marry the man she loves.

Answers on page 164

5. In the best-selling American novel of the nineteenth century, a kindly family falls on hard times and is forced to sell its faithful slave: he goes through a series of owners before being whipped to death by a cruel master.

6. Two men of remarkably similar appearance are caught up in the French Revolution. One falls in love with the other's wife and makes a great sacrifice for her.

7. A poor student murders an elderly pawnbroker and thereafter behaves so strangely that his discovery and conviction become inevitable.

8. A small boy is lost by his parents in the Indian jungle and subsequently brought up by wolves.

9. Several hundred years in the future, people are kept happy by being given mind-altering drugs and categorized as Alphas, Betas, Gammas, etc. according to their station in life. The arrival of The Savage threatens to disturb the harmony of this apparently perfect society.

10. A small boy decides never to grow up. The novel is apparently his autobiography, written when he is in his thirties; he is confined to a mental institution and still in possession of a toy he was given when he was three years old.

Answers on page 164

10 Where Did They All Come From?

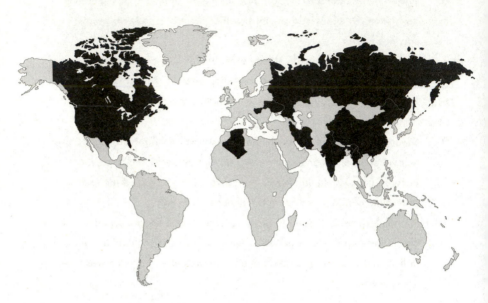

Not all authors lived and worked in the country (or the language) of their birth. Can you match the birthplaces of these authors to the countries marked in black on the map?

1. J. G. Ballard
2. Saul Bellow
3. Albert Camus
4. Joseph Conrad
5. T. S. Eliot
6. Arthur Koestler
7. Doris Lessing
8. Vladimir Nabokov
9. George Orwell
10. Saki (H. H. Munro)

Answers on page 164

11 Shakespeare Summaries

Identify the plays from the descriptions. These are among the Bard's most famous works, so no multiple choice here – just cast your mind back to those old set texts.

1. A Scottish general is accosted by witches, setting in train a series of unfortunate events
2. A lively young woman and a man who has sworn never to marry finally realize they love each other
3. The daughter of an exiled duke disguises herself as a boy in order to join her father in the Forest of Arden
4. The heir to the throne spends most of his time drinking with disreputable companions, including a boastful and cowardly old knight
5. A wife falsely accused of adultery is murdered by her jealous husband
6. An old king asks his daughters how much they love him and is offended by one of the replies
7. A weak king who has allowed his kingdom to fall into disarray is eventually overthrown and killed
8. The fate of two pairs of young lovers is determined by the fairies in a wood near Athens
9. An exiled duke and his daughter live on a lonely island with spirits as their servants
10. A twin brother and sister are separated in a shipwreck; she disguises herself as a boy and enters the service of a duke

Answers on page 165

12 Shakespearean Couples

Match boy to girl in these couples – either lovers or spouses – and then match them to their respective plays.

1. Duke of Albany
2. Antipholus of Ephesus
3. Bassanio
4. Claudius
5. Demetrius
6. Iago
7. Leontes
8. Orsino
9. Petruchio
10. Valentine

A. Adriana
B. Emilia
C. Gertrude
D. Goneril
E. Helena
F. Hermione
G. Katharina
H. Portia
I. Silvia
J. Viola

I.   A Comedy of Errors
II.   Hamlet
III. King Lear
IV.   The Merchant of Venice
V.   A Midsummer Night's Dream
VI.   Othello
VII. The Taming of the Shrew

Answers on page 166

VIII. *Twelfth Night*

IX. *Two Gentlemen of Verona*

X. *A Winter's Tale*

13 Shakespeare Locations

Printed versions of Shakespeare's plays begin (in my edition, anyway) with a line detailing where each one is set. Can you match each play to its location?

1. A city in Illyria and the sea coast near it
2. Vienna
3. Navarre
4. Sometimes in Sicily; sometimes in Bohemia
5. The sea, with a ship; afterwards an uninhabited island
6. At the beginning of the play, England; but afterwards wholly in France
7. Troy, and the Grecian camp before it
8. During a great part of the play at Rome; afterwards at Sardis, and near Philippi
9. Britain
10. Elsinore

A. *Hamlet*
B. *Henry V*
C. *Julius Caesar*
D. *King Lear*
E. *Love's Labour's Lost*
F. *Measure for Measure*
G. *The Tempest*
H. *Troilus and Cressida*
I. *Twelfth Night*
J. *A Winter's Tale*

Answers on page 166

14 Popular Misquotations

This goes back to the 'get it right' theme of the previous chapter. If you quote a famous line wrongly – as we have all been known to do – you can bet your life there will be someone in the room who'll take great pleasure in putting you right. So can you correct the following common misquotations and provide the sources?

To help you, there are four from Shakespeare, two from the Bible and four from other sources – one of which, although it's a very familiar quotation, is likely to be someone you have never heard of.

1. A poor thing, but mine own.
2. A prophet is without honour in his own country.
3. Blood, sweat and tears.
4. Discretion is the better part of valour.
5. 'Elementary, my dear Watson.'
6. Hell hath no fury like a woman scorned.
7. Now is the winter of our discontent.
8. Power corrupts.
9. There's nothing new under the sun.
10. To gild the lily.

15 Other Playwrights

Yes, they do exist. You may even have studied some of them. See if you can match the plays to the playwrights and to the dates of their first performance.

1. *Death of a Salesman*
2. *Doctor Faustus*
3. *The Duchess of Malfi*
4. *An Ideal Husband*
5. *Look Back in Anger*
6. *Our Town*
7. *The Rivals*
8. *Saint Joan*
9. *A Streetcar Named Desire*
10. *The Way of the World*

A. William Congreve
B. Christopher Marlowe
C. Arthur Miller
D. John Osborne
E. George Bernard Shaw
F. Richard Brinsley Sheridan
G. John Webster
H. Oscar Wilde
I. Thornton Wilder
J. Tennessee Williams

I. 1592
II. 1623
III. 1700
IV. 1775
V. 1895
VI. 1923
VII. 1938
VIII. 1947
IX. 1949
X. 1956

Answers on page 168

16 Austen Marriages

Jane Austen's heroes are rarely referred to by their first names, but can you identify them anyway and link them to their books?

1. If Fitzwilliam marries Elizabeth, whom does William marry? And what about George and Charles?
2. If Frank marries Jane, whom does George marry?
3. If John is married to Fanny, whom do Edward and Christopher marry?
4. If Charles is married to Mary, whom does Frederick marry?
5. If James's heart is broken by Isabella, whom does Henry marry?
6. If Maria elopes with Henry, whom does Edmund marry?

And, while we're on the subject of Jane Austen, can you list, in chronological order, the novels that were published in her lifetime? The answer may surprise you.

17 Complete the quotation

What is needed now is the missing word of the famous quotation, the poem from which it comes and the author. They're all here, but can you match them up?

1. All in the —— of death rode the six hundred
2. From the —— he named her, Minnehaha, Laughing Water
3. If you can meet with —— and Disaster
4. In England's green and pleasant ——
5. Look on my ——, ye mighty, and despair
6. Much have I travelled in the realms of ——
7. That is no —— for old men

8. There's some —— of a foreign field that is for ever England
9. What passing-bells for these who die as ——?
10. Where Alph, the sacred river, ran through —— measureless to man

A. cattle
B. caverns
C. corner
D. country
E. gold
F. land
G. triumph
H. valley
I. waterfall
J. works

I. 'Anthem for Doomed Youth'
II. 'The Charge of the Light Brigade'
III. 'If——'
IV. 'Jerusalem'
V. 'Kubla Khan'
VI. 'On First Looking into Chapman's Homer'
VII. 'Ozymandias'
VIII. 'Sailing to Byzantium'
IX. 'The Soldier'
X. *The Song of Hiawatha*

1. William Blake
2. Rupert Brooke
3. Samuel Taylor Coleridge
4. John Keats
5. Rudyard Kipling
6. Henry Wadsworth Longfellow
7. Wilfred Owen
8. Percy Bysshe Shelley
9. Alfred, Lord Tennyson
10. W. B. Yeats

Answers on page 169

18 And Again . . .

Complete the quotation. This time they are all from Shakespeare, so you need to fill in the gap and match the quotation to the play and the speaker.

1. A —— o' both your houses!
2. For in that sleep of —— what dreams may come
3. If —— be the food of love, play on
4. Love looks not with the eyes but with the ——
5. Is this a —— which I see before me?
6. O brave new ——, that has such people in't.
7. The barge she sat in, like a burnish'd ——
8. The —— that men do lives after them
9. This blessed plot, this earth, this ——, this England
10. What, my dear lady ——! Are you yet living?

A. Dagger
B. Death
C. Disdain
D. Evil
E. Mind
F. Music
G. Plague
H. Realm
I. Throne
J. World

I.   *Antony and Cleopatra*
II. *Hamlet*
III. *Julius Caesar*
IV. *Macbeth*
V.   *A Midsummer Night's Dream*
VI. *Much Ado About Nothing*

VII. *Richard II*

VIII. *Romeo and Juliet*

IX. *The Tempest*

X. *Twelfth Night*

1. Benedick
2. Enobarbus
3. Hamlet
4. Helena
5. John of Gaunt
6. Macbeth
7. Mark Antony
8. Mercutio
9. Miranda
10. Orsino

Answers on page 169

3 HISTORY

Kings, queens, presidents, prime ministers and all those clever people who discovered continents or invented steam engines – that is what this chapter is about. And, because it's history, there's rather a lot of dates, too. See how good you are at remembering not only who did what, but when they did it.

1 Divorced, Beheaded, Died . . .

A bit of a cliché, this one, but it would look odd to leave it out. So, can you name the six wives of Henry VIII in order, and link them to the fates described in the rhyme?

And, just to make it a bit more challenging, can you then rank them in order of how long each was Queen of England?

2 Which Came First?

Since 1066, there have been nine royal houses of England (and subsequently the United Kingdom). Here they are in alphabetical order; can you put them in chronological order and, for bonus points, give their dates and their first and last monarchs?

1. Hanover
2. Lancaster
3. Normandy
4. Plantagenet
5. Saxe-Coburg-Gotha
6. Stuart
7. Tudor
8. Windsor
9. York

Answers on page 170

3 Which Came First 2?

And try the same with American presidents and Canadian prime ministers: put the following in chronological order and give yourself extra points if you know the year they were first inaugurated or elected. Clue: they were all in office in the twentieth century.

1. Calvin Coolidge
2. Dwight D. Eisenhower
3. John F. Kennedy
4. Mackenzie King
5. Lester Pearson
6. Ronald Reagan
7. Franklin D. Roosevelt
8. Theodore Roosevelt
9. Pierre Trudeau
10. Woodrow Wilson

Answers on page 171

4 Let Battle Commence!

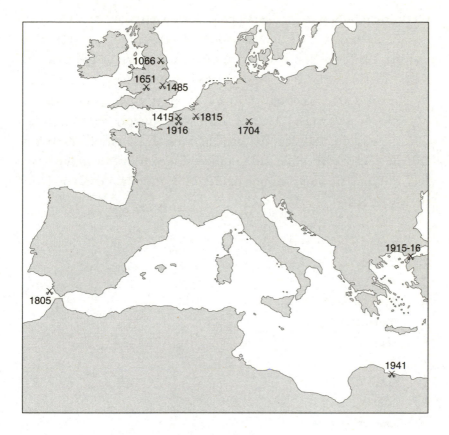

The map shows ten significant battles in European and world history. Can you name them and also the conflicts of which they were part?

Answers on page 171

5 Where Will It All End?

Of course most monarchs die in office: the job tends to be for life. The exceptions to this rule have been forcibly removed for one reason or another. Presidents and prime ministers – in democratic countries, at least – are elected for a fixed term, which most of them survive.

But there are exceptions to this as to every rule. So here's a list of twelve world leaders. Half of them were forcibly removed from office – assassinated, deposed or otherwise disposed of; the other half died peacefully while still in office. Can you sort them into two lists, then put them into chronological order with their dates of death or deposition?

1. Edward II
2. Edward IV
3. Indira Gandhi
4. James Garfield
5. Warren Harding
6. Emperor Hirohito
7. Louis XIV
8. Louis XVI
9. Tsar Nicholas II
10. Spencer Perceval
11. William Pitt the Younger
12. Franklin D. Roosevelt

Answers on page 172

6 Line of Succession

Here are five lists of British monarchs who ruled consecutively. One name has been omitted from each sequence. Fill in the gaps from the suggestions provided – but note that there are six possibilities. One of them is a red herring.

1. William II, Henry I, ——, Henry II
2. Richard I, John, ——, Edward I
3. ——, Henry IV, Henry V, Henry VI
4. Edward VI, ——, Elizabeth I, James I
5. George III, George IV, ——, Victoria

A. Henry III
B. Mary I
C. Richard II
D. Stephen
E. William III
F. William IV

And try the same thing with American presidents; again, one is a red herring:

1. John Adams, Thomas Jefferson, ——, James Monroe
2. John Quincy Adams, ——, Martin von Buren, William Henry Harrison
3. Franklin Pierce, ——, Abraham Lincoln, Andrew Johnson
4. Grover Cleveland, Benjamin Harrison, ——, William McKinley
5. Woodrow Wilson, Warren G. Harding, Calvin Coolidge, ——

A. James Buchanan
B. Grover Cleveland
C. Herbert Hoover
D. Andrew Jackson
E. James Madison
F. William Howard Taft

Answers on page 173

7 Commonwealth Prime Ministers

Match the following names to the countries where they held office and put them in chronological order.

1. Sirimavo Bandaranaike
2. John Diefenbaker
3. Lee Kuan Yew
4. Robert Menzies
5. Robert Muldoon
6. Jawaharlal Nehru
7. Kwame Nkrumah
8. Julius Nyerere
9. Milton Obote
10. Hendrik Verwoerd

A. Australia
B. Canada
C. Ceylon/Sri Lanka
D. Ghana
E. India
F. New Zealand
G. Singapore
H. South Africa
I. Tanzania
J. Uganda

8 A Royal Family Tree (or Two)

Can you identify A and B in these two (unconnected) family trees? All were reigning monarchs in some country or other.

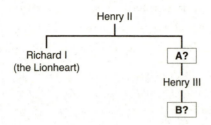

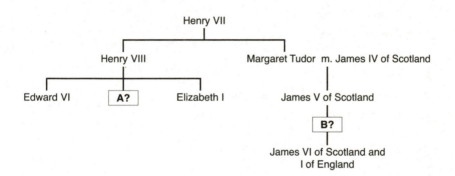

9 Royal Spouses

Who married whom? Match the consorts in the first list to the monarchs in the second (the monarchs are kings of England or of the United Kingdom unless stated). And, just for fun, have a go at the dates of the weddings. Give yourself points if you get within ten years and remember that the marriages often took place before the groom became king.

1. Anne of Denmark
2. Anne Neville
3. Caroline of Brunswick
4. Eleanor of Aquitaine
5. Eleanor of Castile
6. Eleanor of Provence
7. Henrietta Maria of France
8. Marie Antoinette
9. Marie des Médicis (Maria de' Medici)
10. Mary of Teck

A. Charles I
B. Edward I
C. George IV
D. George V
E. Henri IV of France
F. Henry II
G. Henry III
H. James VI and I
I. Louis XVI of France
J. Richard III

10 Because It Was There

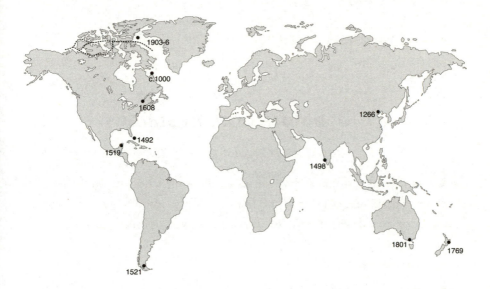

Look at the map. Can you link the places and explorers in the lists below to the sites and dates shown on the map?

1. Cape Kidnappers
2. Melbourne
3. Straits of Magellan
4. Yucatán Peninsula
5. Quebec
6. Northwest Passage
7. Northern tip of Newfoundland
8. Bahamas
9. Calicut
10. Beijing

A. Roald Amundsen
B. Samuel de Champlain
C. Christopher Columbus
D. James Cook
E. Hernán Cortés

Answers on page 175

F. Leif Ericson

G. Ferdinand Magellan

H. Matthew Flinders

I. Marco Polo

J. Vasco da Gama

11 Inventors and Inventions

Match the inventions or discoveries to the men who invented them, discovered them, got in first with the patent or in some other way came to be associated with them. Then put them into chronological order.

1. Archimedes

2. Charles Babbage

3. Roger Bacon

4. Thomas Edison

5. Alexander Fleming

6. Benjamin Franklin

7. Johannes Gutenberg

8. James Hargreaves

9. Guglielmo Marconi

10. Jethro Tull

A. The analytical engine, a forerunner of the computer

B. Bifocals

C. An irrigation device that bears the inventor's name

D. The light bulb

E. The magnifying glass

F. Movable type printing

G. Penicillin

H. An early seed drill

I. The spinning jenny

J. Wireless telegraphy

Answers on page 175–6

12 What the Romans Did for Us

And the Chinese, for that matter. The following list contains five inventions generally attributed to the ancient Romans (or to clever Greeks working in the Roman Empire) and five for which the Chinese get the credit. Can you separate them?

A coin-operated vending machine

Concrete

The fire engine

Fireworks

The magnetic compass

The oar

The odometer

Paper

Playing cards

Underfloor heating

Answers on page 176

13 Renaissance Movers and Shakers

Match the names to the CVs, then put them into chronological order

1. Filippo Brunelleschi
2. John Calvin
3. Benvenuto Cellini
4. Nicolas Copernicus
5. Desiderius Erasmus
6. Martin Luther
7. Niccolò Machiavelli
8. Lorenzo de' Medici
9. Francesco Petrarch
10. William Tyndale

A. Architect responsible for the dome of Florence cathedral.

B. Dutch scholar and humanist whose criticism of the Church raised questions that would be influential in the Protestant Reformation.

C. Florentine politician whose name is associated with a ruthless belief in the end justifying the means.

D. French theologian largely based in Geneva, a firm believer in predestination and hugely influential in the development of the Protestant church, notably of Presbyterianism.

E. German priest, one of the most important figures of the Reformation, who protested against the practice of paying money so that God would forgive sins.

F. Italian goldsmith who also wrote a racy autobiography confessing to several murders.

G. Member of a fabulously wealthy banking family in Florence and a patron of, among others, Botticelli and Michelangelo.

H. Poet who developed a form of sonnet that survives to this day; also instrumental in preserving many classical texts and dubbed 'the Father of the Renaissance' .

I. Polish mathematician and astronomer, one of the first to maintain that the earth both rotated on its own axis and orbited the sun.

J. Prominent figure in the English Reformation, made the first translations of parts of the Bible into English.

14 Column Inches

Different styles of architecture are given different names depending on where they originated or who first designed or popularized them. Match the illustrations to the styles listed below.

1. Composite
2. Corinthian
3. Doric

Answers on page 176–7

4. Gothic

5. Ionic

6. Norman

7. Palladian

8. Roman

15 Time Line of Unfortunate Events

History is full of unfortunate events: natural disasters, wars and uprisings, bad people getting into power. Can you match the following happenings to the dates on the time line?

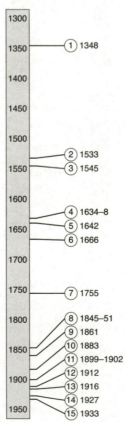

1. Adolf Hitler becomes Chancellor of Germany.
2. The Battle of Edge Hill marks the beginning of the English Civil War.
3. The Black Death ravages Europe.
4. The Boer War is one of the earliest in which concentration camps are used.
5. The bombardment of Fort Sumter starts the American Civil War.
6. Captain Scott and his party die in Antarctica after losing the race to be first to the South Pole.
7. The Easter Rising ends with sixteen Irish leaders being executed.
8. The Great Famine kills a million people in Ireland and forces many to emigrate.
9. The Great Fire of London destroys much of the city.
10. In Indonesia, the volcanic island of Krakatoa erupts, killing tens of thousands of people.
11. Ivan the Terrible becomes the first Tsar of Russia.
12. Josef Stalin becomes Soviet leader.
13. Lisbon is destroyed by the most powerful earthquake ever recorded at the time.
14. The Pequot War decimates the Native American people after whom it is named.
15. The warship *Mary Rose* sinks off the south coast of England.

Answers on page 177

16 But It Wasn't All Bad

Sometimes good things happen too: great works of art are created, civil liberties are extended, brilliant minds push back the frontiers of science. See how you get on attaching the good news to the appropriate dates.

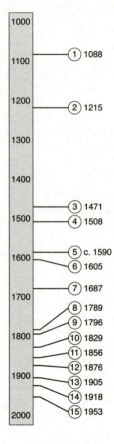

A. After her experience of nursing during the Crimean War, Florence Nightingale establishes an institution for the training of nurses.

B. Albert Einstein proposes his Special Theory of Relativity.

C. Alexander Graham Bell patents the telephone.

D. The Bill of Rights, consisting of ten amendments to the American Constitution, is adopted.

E. Edward Jenner carries out the first vaccination against smallpox.

F. Francis Watson and James Crick construct a molecular model of DNA.

G. Guy Fawkes and others fail to blow up the Houses of Parliament (let's pretend we think this is good news).

H. Isaac Newton publishes his three laws of motion.

I. Magna Carta paves the way for democratic government by limiting the monarch's powers.

J. Michelangelo agrees to work on the ceiling of the Sistine Chapel.

K. Shakespeare writes his first surviving play.

L. Stephenson's 'Rocket' reaches 36 miles (58.5 km) an hour and becomes a landmark in the development of railways.

M. William Caxton issues the first book in English to be printed from movable type.

N. Women over the age of thirty are granted the vote in the UK.

O. The world's first university is founded in Bologna.

Answers on page 178

4 GEOGRAPHY

Contrary to what outsiders may believe, geography isn't all about places on a map. It can range over geology, meteorology, economics, sociology and lots more besides. However, it's not easy to work an oxbow lake into tests of this kind, so you'll find that this chapter does in fact contain quite a few maps – and that I have asked you to mark places on them.

1 Name That Town

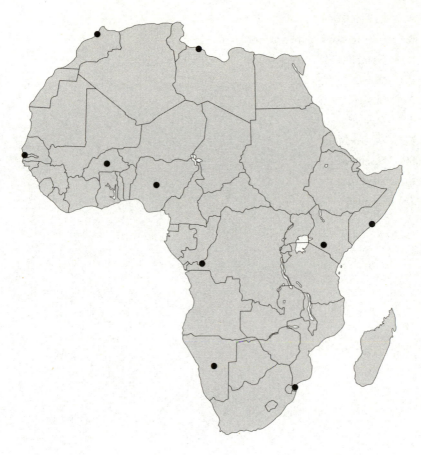

The map shows ten African capital cities. Can you match the cities to their countries and then mark them on the map?

1.   Abuja
2.   Banjul
3.   Kinshasa
4.   Maputo
5.   Mogadishu
6.   Nairobi
7.   Ouagadougou

Answers on page 179

8. Rabat

9. Tripoli

10. Windhoek

A. Burkina Faso

B. Democratic Republic of the Congo

C. Gambia

D. Kenya

E. Libya

F. Morocco

G. Mozambique

H. Namibia

I. Nigeria

J. Somalia

Answers on page 179

2 Name That Town 2

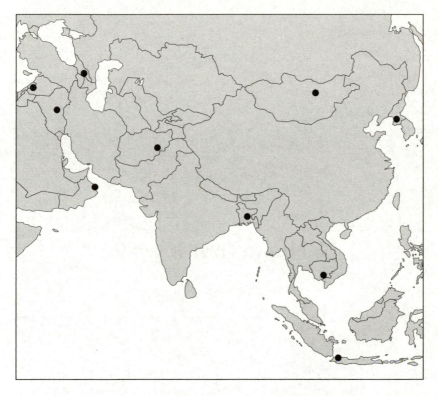

Too easy? Too hard? Try again with Asia. Match capital to country and identify them on the map.

1. Baghdad
2. Damascus
3. Dhaka
4. Djakarta
5. Kabul
6. Muscat
7. Phnom Penh
8. Pyongyang
9. Tbilisi

Answers on page 180

10. Ulan Bator

A. Afghanistan

B. Bangladesh

C. Cambodia

D. Georgia

E. Indonesia

F. Iraq

G. Mongolia

H. North Korea

I. Oman

J. Syria

3 Name That Town 3

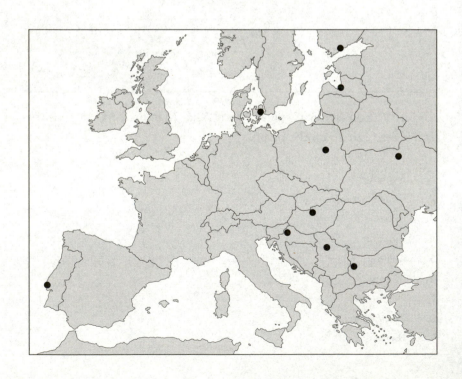

And again with Europe.

1. Belgrade
2. Budapest
3. Copenhagen
4. Helsinki
5. Kiev
6. Lisbon
7. Riga
8. Sofia
9. Warsaw
10. Zagreb

A. Bulgaria
B. Croatia
C. Denmark
D. Finland
E. Hungary
F. Latvia
G. Poland
H. Portugal
I. Serbia
J. Ukraine

Answers on page 181

4 US State Capitals

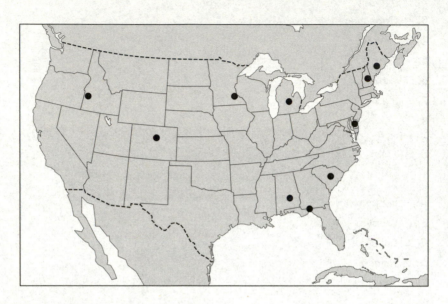

This time, match the capitals to the states, and mark on the map:

1. Augusta
2. Boise
3. Columbia
4. Concord
5. Denver
6. Dover
7. Lansing
8. Montgomery
9. St Paul
10. Tallahassee

A. Alabama
B. Colorado
C. Delaware
D. Florida

Answers on page 182

E. Idaho

F. Maine

G. Michigan

H. Minnesota

I. New Hampshire

J. West Virginia

5 (Nick-)Name That State

American states have some weird and wonderful nicknames connected with their history, geography, climate and even tourist attractions. Can you link the nickname to the state and, for extra points, turn back to the previous page and mark those states on the map?

1. Bay State
2. Beehive State
3. Bluegrass State
4. Constitution State
5. Evergreen State
6. Golden State
7. Grand Canyon State
8. Keystone State
9. Mount Rushmore State
10. Volunteer State

A. Arizona
B. California
C. Connecticut
D. Kentucky
E. Massachusetts
F. Pennsylvania
G. South Dakota

Answers on page 182–3

H.   Tennessee

I.   Utah

J.   Washington

6 O Canada!

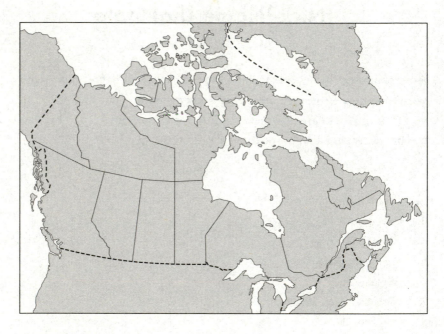

The world's second largest country is divided into ten provinces and three territories: can you mark them on the map?

1.   Alberta

2.   British Columbia

3.   Manitoba

4.   New Brunswick

5.   Newfoundland

6.   Northwest Territories

7.   Nova Scotia

8. Nunavut
9. Ontario
10. Prince Edward Island
11. Quebec
12. Saskatchewan
13. Yukon

7 Australia Fair

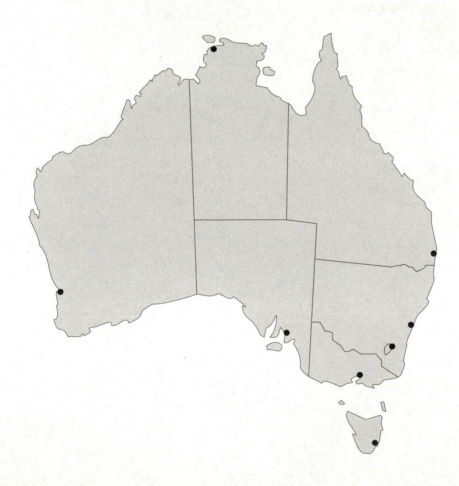

Answers on page 184–5

Australia has, for most practical purposes, six states and two territories. (I'm sure there is a 'Freedom for Jervis Bay' movement out their somewhere, but I am not going to let it complicate this quiz.) Mark them on the map and link them to their capitals.

1. Australian Capital Territory
2. New South Wales
3. Northern Territory
4. Queensland
5. South Australia
6. Tasmania
7. Victoria
8. Western Australia

A. Adelaide
B. Brisbane
C. Canberra
D. Darwin
E. Hobart
F. Melbourne
G. Perth
H. Sydney

Answers on page 185

8 Spoken Here

Many countries across the world have a European language as their 'official' language: a souvenir, if that is the word I want, of colonial times. Others have adopted local tribal languages either as well or instead, and have a number of official languages, reflecting their racial mix. So can you match the following languages to the countries where they are spoken?

Note that I have not always listed all the languages that a country recognizes.

1.   Amharic
2.   Arabic, French
3.   Catalan, Galician
4.   English, Tagalog
5.   English, Tswana, Xhosa
6.   English, Urdu
7.   English, Yoruba
8.   French, German, Italian
9.   Greek, Turkish
10. Spanish, Quechua, Aymara

A.   Chad
B.   Cyprus
C.   Ethiopia
D.   Nigeria
E.   Pakistan
F.   Peru
G.   Philippines
H.   South Africa
I.   Spain
J.   Switzerland

Answers on page 186

9 Climb Every Mountain . . .

The highest mountains on each of the world's seven continents are:

Aconcagua

Blanc

Everest

Kilimanjaro

McKinley

Vinson Massif

Wilhelm

Can you assign each one to its continent? (No, I'm not giving you a list: think them up for yourself.) Then put them in order of height and – for lots of extra points – have a guess at those heights.

Answers on page 186

10 . . . Ford Every Stream

Can you identify these rivers and put them in order of length? They include the five longest in the world and five others.

1. Amazon
2. Danube
3. Mackenzie
4. Mekong
5. Mississippi-Missouri
6. Murray-Darling
7. Nile
8. Paraná-Plate
9. Yangtze
10. Yenisey-Angara

Answers on page 187

11 Oceans, Seas and Lakes

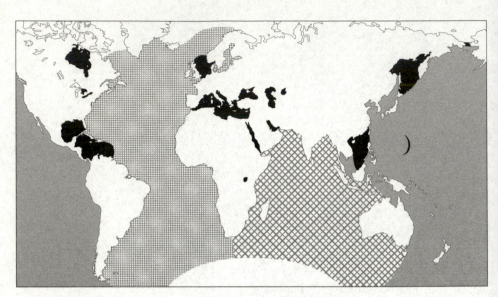

Over two-thirds of our planet is covered in the stuff, but can you label the following bodies of water?

OCEANS

1. Atlantic
2. Indian
3. Pacific

SEAS

4. Aral
5. Black
6. Caspian
7. Caribbean
8. Mediterranean
9. North
10. Okhotsk (never heard of it? Shame on you! It's the sixth largest sea in the world.)

11. Red
12. South China

LAKES

13. Erie
14. Huron
15. Victoria

OTHERS

16. Bering Strait
17. Gulf of Mexico
18. Hudson Bay
19. Mariana Trench (at 11,022 metres, the deepest point in the world)
20. Persian Gulf

Answers on page 188

12 The Age of the Dinosaurs

Not just dinosaurs, but other ancient creatures. Despite what you might have gleaned from *Jurassic Park*, these creatures existed over a period of many millions of years and weren't all alive at the same time. Can you identify the animal from the drawing, assign it to the period when it first appeared and put those periods into chronological order?

Note that 'period' is a technical term in geological timelines, but I am using it in its everyday sense: some of the periods listed below should, strictly speaking, be described as epochs.

1. Ammonite
2. *Coelophysis*
3. *Diplodocus*
4. Mammoth
5. Sabre-toothed cat
6. *Tyrannosaurus rex*

A. Cretaceous

B. Devonian

C. Eocene

D. Jurassic

E. Pliocene

F. Triassic

13 Pick a Cloud

Match the illustration to the cloud type and then to the definition.

1. Cirrus

2. Cumulonimbus

3. Cumulus

4. Nimbostratus

5. Stratus

A. Dark, three-dimensional clouds associated with bad weather.

B. Flat, uniform, greyish clouds that seem to cover the whole sky.

Answers on page 189–90

C. Shapeless clouds that are all the harder to make out because it is probably raining.

D. Thin wisps of cloud very high in the sky.

E. White, fluffy clouds, often seen on a fine day.

14 Yes, of Course I Know What That Is . . .

Geography is full of semi-technical terms that we sort of understand: can you come up with the terms that are being defined here?

1. A body of seawater almost entirely cut off from the ocean by a barrier beach or coral reef.

2. A large volcanic crater formed by the collapse of a volcano following an eruption.

3. A neck of land connecting two larger landmasses.

4. A ring of coral forming an island or group of islands.

5. A seasonal wind that brings heavy rain to southern Asia.

6. A strong, cold wind felt in southern France and in the Mediterranean.

7. Any chain or group of islands.

8. Predictable winds blowing towards the equator.

9. Superheated rock beneath the earth's surface.

10. What used inaccurately to be called a tidal wave – a massive sea wave caused by an earthquake or similar activity.

5 MATHS

When I first wrote I Used to Know That, *I was surprised to discover that maths was the subject most people wanted to talk about, even though (or perhaps because) it was the one with the most dreadful memories from school days. So, at the risk of regenerating some of those old nightmares, let's see how you do . . .*

NON-CALCULATOR

To start with, here are some calculations to work out the way our ancestors did them – on paper or in your head.

1 What's (or Where's) the Point?

Decimal points can pose some nasty traps if you don't remember the basic rule. See if you can recapture the decimal-point agility you developed back in the day . . .

A. 0.8 x 0.4

B. 1.2 x 0.04

C. 1.1 x 1.1 x 1.1

D. 1.1 x 2.2 x 3.3

2 Scary Fractions

Remember lowest common multiples? Of course you do. The first part of this test might seem irrelevant, but trust me . . .

A. Find 11x13

B. Factorize these two numbers into prime factors:

208

352

C. Find their lowest common multiple [LCM(208, 352)]

Answers on page 191

D. Find exactly, as a single fraction (remember, no calculator):

$$\frac{3}{208} - \frac{5}{352}$$

3 Monty Hall

This is a famous probability problem that stumped a lot of professional mathematicians when it was published in 1975 (inspired by a TV show, no less, and named after the show's host). It makes use of basic probability just like that which you learned at school – and still for most people its solution is fiendishly counter-intuitive. Here goes:

You're on a game show, and you have a choice of three doors to open. Behind one is a nice prize and behind the other two are lumps of coal. You're asked to choose a door, but not to open it. Once you have done so the host opens one of the two doors you didn't pick to reveal a lump of coal. She can do this because she knows which door the prize is behind. Now she offers you a choice. You can stick to your original choice of door and win what is behind that, or you can change your mind and win what is behind the remaining mystery door. What should you do to give yourself the best chance of winning the prize?

Answers on page 191–2

4 Accent-u-ate the Negative

Negative signs, don't you just love them? Let's see how you are at combining negative and positive in these sums:

A. $-1 + 4$

B. $3 - -2$

C. $\dfrac{6}{-3}$

D. $\dfrac{(-2+7)}{-5}$

E. $3 \times (-2) + \dfrac{14}{-7} - \dfrac{15}{(-3-2)}$

5 At the Same Time . . .

Time to decipher one of those exam favourites, the wordy simultaneous equations question...

Three years ago, Constance was twice Charlie's age. In one year she'll be nine years older than he is now. How old is Charlie? How old is Constance?

6 Venn Diagram Fun

I ask 100 people in a strange village about their pets: do they have snakes, dogs or rabbits? Where I say '29 people have snakes' I mean they have at least one snake – for the purposes of this exercise it doesn't matter how many of each species they possess. Here's what I find:

1. 29 people have snakes
2. 34 people have rabbits
3. 7 people have snakes and rabbits
4. 70% of the people have at least one of the three animals
5. 30% of the people have dogs but no rabbits
6. 60% of the people have snakes and/or dogs
7. There are twice the number of people owning snakes and dogs as there are people owning rabbits and only rabbits.

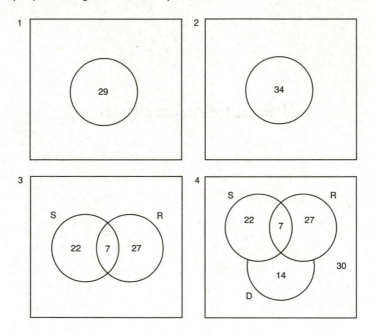

Start to collate this information as shown, with S, R and D standing for snakes, rabbits and dogs, and see if you can work out how many people own all three – snakes, dogs and rabbits?

Answers on page 193

7 Get It Done by Friday

Stuck on a desert island with no calculator? Want to get a job as an engineer for the indigenous people? Better quickly recall all that long-winded arithmetic from school!

A.   32010 x 4100

B.   9999 x 99

C.   Divide 28613 by 71

D.   Divide 131.573 by 1.3

8 Fraction Acrobatics

Express the following as single simplified fractions:

A. $\dfrac{7}{2+\frac{1}{3}}$

B. $\dfrac{\frac{1}{2}-\frac{1}{3}}{\frac{1}{4}}$

C. $1+\dfrac{1}{\dfrac{1+1}{2+\frac{1}{3}}}$

D. $1-(\frac{1}{2}+\frac{1}{4}+\frac{1}{8}+\frac{1}{16})$

9 Hired or Fired?

Here's another of those wordy brainteasers that test your understanding of percentages and algebra.

Martha sells jars of jam at a farmers' market. She has 80 jars to sell at £3 each.

She sells 50 jars, then reduces the price by 40% and sells the remaining jars at the reduced price.

It costs her £95 to make the jars of jam. Her target is to make a profit of at least £100. Does she do it?

10 Mean, Median and Mode

Do you remember the different types of average? Time to dig up those M-words!

The heights in centimetres of a group of fifteen 10-year-olds are given below (in ascending order). Calculate the mean, median and mode of this sample:

126, 133, 133, 135, 135, 136, 138, 140, 140, 141, 145, 145, 145, 147, 148

Answers on page 195

CALCULATOR

Okay, into the twenty-first century. You're allowed to use that little machine to help you with this section.

11 A Question of Scale

Do you remember how ratios of length affect ratios of area and volume?

If I own a swimming pool that is in the same proportions as yours, but yours is twice as long, how much more water can you fit in yours than in mine?

The radius of the earth (the distance from the centre to the crust) is about 3.67 times that of the moon. If I have a giant flexible blanket which can cover 1/3 of the surface of the moon, how much of the surface of the earth can it cover?

12 Sine Rule

Once upon a time you could probably recite the 'sine rule' if suddenly woken and held at water-pistol-point at 3 a.m. But how about now? And can you use it to solve this conundrum?

Ralph has a piece of apparatus for measuring the angle above the ground of objects he can see in the distance. He also has a 'wheel on a stick' accurately measuring how far he walks (assuming he can do it in a straight line!). He's considering climbing a hill he sees in the distance. Spotting a particularly interesting tree at the top of the hill, he measures the tree as being 15 degrees above the ground. He then walks 100m directly towards the hill and measures the tree at 16 degrees above the ground.

How tall is the hill?

Answers on page 196

13 How High the Cone?

Here's something else to test your memory of trigonometry.

Oihana is in the jungle building a hut using bamboo. She leans sticks of bamboo symmetrically to make a cone shape, something like a tepee:

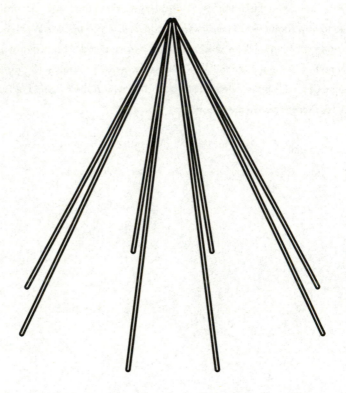

The base of a cone is by definition circular (you knew that, didn't you?). The sticks are 6m long from the ground to where they meet at the peak of the hut. Oihana measures the angle that one of the sticks makes with the ground (they all make the same angle, because she is very skilled) at 60 degrees.

A.   How tall is the hut?

B.   What is the diameter of the floor of the hut?

C.   Assuming the hut is a perfect cone (Oihana really is very skilled), what is the volume inside it?

14 Pythagoras

Ever wondered when all that 'square on the hypotenuse' business would come in useful? Well, here you are.

Farmer James has a bull in a rectangular enclosure measuring 50m x 75m. He is standing inside the (diagonally) opposite corner to a lone bull, Fenton, who dislikes James and decides to charge at him along the diagonal. Fenton runs at 8m per second. How long does James have to climb out of harm's way?

15 Declaring an Interest

Remember simple and compound interest? Here's an example of both.

A.   You have £30. I want to borrow it, and offer you 1% per day interest on the loan. If you want to make at least £1 from me, how many days would you hope it takes me before I pay you back?

B.   Paolo started a savings account 5 years ago, when he deposited all the money he had in his hat. After 2 years the bank dropped his annual rate of interest from 4% to 3%. He now has £2377.97 in that account. How much money did he have in his hat 5 years ago?

Answers on page 197

16 I Wish It Could Be Christmas Every Day

A company makes 400 Christmas toys.

Each toy costs £4.70 to make.

One-quarter of the toys are given away to a children's home.

Three-fifths of the rest are sold for the full price of £12.

The remainder are sold at half price.

How much profit does the company make?

17 All's Fair . . .

For me, and I'll bet many of you, understanding probability started out with tossing fair coins and rolling fair dice. In life not all is fair, and these simple probabilities provide a comforting retreat for nerds and poker-players alike. Enjoy.

A.   I toss a fair coin twice. What's the probability that I get exactly one head?

B.   I toss a fair coin four times. What's the probability that I get exactly two tails?

C.   I roll a pair of fair dice. What's the probability that my total score is four?

D.   I roll three fair dice. What's the probability that my total score is four?

6 SCIENCE

Somehow this seems to be the subject many of us miss out on: even the most hardened scientists learn a bit of English, but very little science seeps into the general knowledge of those who study arts or humanities. We even lump a number of subjects together and call them 'general science', allowing us to skate over the surface of quite a wide area. So this is an extra-long chapter because it encompasses the three main science subjects — biology, chemistry and physics.

BIOLOGY

From the Greek meaning the study of life, *this covers how plants breathe (photosynthesis), how we breathe (respiration) and how, as long as we keep breathing, the rest of our functions . . . well . . . function. Ready for a bit of reproduction, circulation and fermentation? Read on.*

1 Cell Reproduction

Within our bodies, and everywhere else for that matter, cell reproduction is constantly happening. As our organs grow or muscles repair themselves, cells we already have are copied as a contribution towards producing tissue. When we reproduce, we need to 'shuffle' our DNA, split our 'deck' into two halves, and mix half of our deck with half of someone else's to create a whole new genetic make-up for our offspring. Can you match up the 'sciency' names for all this?

1.	Mitosis	**A.**	A cell containing 2 complete sets of chromosomes, one from each parent.
2.	Meiosis	**B.**	The process of one diploid cell dividing into 2 genetically identical diploid cells.
3.	Haploid Cell	**C.**	The process of one diploid cell dividing into 4 genetically unique haploid cells.
4.	Diploid Cell	**D.**	A cell containing 1 complete set of chromosomes.

2 Gene Talk

Match these words to their meanings. It'll be useful when you come to the next question.

1.	Genotype	**A.**	Genetic makeup of a cell, usually with reference to a particular observable trait.
2.	Phenotype	**B.**	Term used when both alleles are the same.
3.	Allele	**C.**	Term used when 2 different alleles are present.
4.	Homozygous	**D.**	An observed characteristic resulting from genetic makeup.
5.	Heterozygous	**E.**	One of 2 or more forms of a gene of group of genes (we have 2 for every gene).

Answers on page 199

3 Baby Blue-Eyes

Now that we have the vocabulary sorted out, let's give it some practical application. Trying to figure out if your kids will have blue eyes? Here's a simple example, assuming that parents-to-be Sarah and Michael's families deal only in recessive blue alleles and dominant brown alleles.

Sarah's dad has blue eyes. Sarah has brown eyes. Michael has blue eyes. What is the probability that their child-to-be will have blue eyes?

4 The Flow of Blood

Remember the difference between arteries and veins? Let's check up on some facts to do with blood flow in the respiratory system.

A.   Is oxygenated blood mostly carried by veins or arteries?

B.   What distinguishes veins from arteries?

C.   What is the main artery distributing oxygenated blood from the heart to the rest of the body?

D.   Name a group of arteries that carry deoxygenated blood. Which organs do they carry blood from/to?

E.   How about a group of veins that carry oxygenated blood? Which organs do they carry blood from/to?

5 A Spoonful of Sugar

Here's some essential information if you know anyone with diabetes. Can you fill in the gaps?

Insulin is a —— produced in the —— which is used to control the level of —— in the blood. When a high level of glucose is detected in the blood, —— is released to lower the levels of glucose by promoting its conversion into —— by cells in the liver, muscle and fat tissue.

glucose, glycogen, hormone, insulin, pancreas

Answers on page 200

6 A Rose Is a Rose . . .

A rose may well be a rose, but what are the different components that make it a flower? Take this list of 'parts' and indicate each one on the diagram:

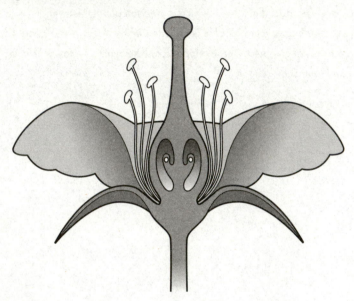

A. Anther

B. Carpel

C. Filament

D. Ovary

E. Ovule

F. Petal

G. Stigma

H. Style

7 Where the Heart Is

Label this diagram of a human heart:

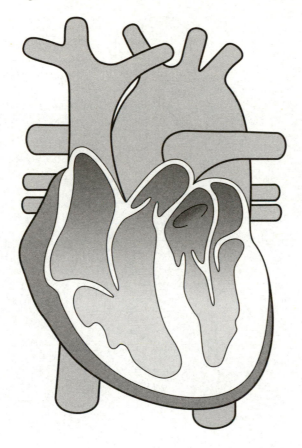

A. Aorta

B. Left atrium

C. Left ventricle

D. Pulmonary artery

E. Right atrium

F. Right ventricle

Answers on page 206

8 You Are What You Eat

Put the labels for these parts of the digestive system in the correct place:

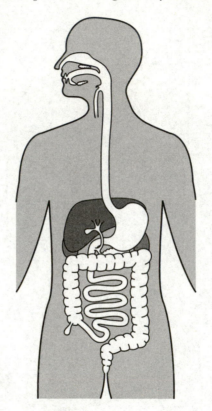

A. Anus

B. Gall bladder

C. Large intestine

D. Liver

E. Oesophagus

F. Pancreas

G. Rectum

H. Salivary glands

I. Small intestine

J. Stomach

9 The Air That We Breathe

As humans, our fuel for living is food. We turn food into energy (and some other things) through respiration. Can you fit the words into this illustrative equation for aerobic respiration?

_____ + _____ → _____ + _____ + _____

water, oxygen, food, energy, carbon dioxide

And, in case that was too easy, can you name another type of respiration and explain the difference between it and aerobic respiration?

10 Fermentation

One well-known and fortunate fact about yeast is that under the right conditions it turns sugar into ethanol (the essence of booze). Put some yeast in a glucose solution, seal it and keep it warm. As the yeast breeds it uses up all the oxygen and then embarks on anaerobic respiration in order to keep going. It then kills itself with alcohol poisoning so that we can do the same.

Can you fit the words into this illustrative equation to describe this process of fermentation?

_____ → _____ + _____ + _____

carbon dioxide, energy, ethanol, glucose

Answers on page 203

11 Animal Cells vs Plant Cells

Do you know the differences between them? Try filling in the blanks in this sentence, using the words supplied:

——cells contain ——, which conduct —— to make food from light, carbon dioxide and water. They have a —— cell wall made of ——.

——cells, on the other hand, are surrounded by only a —— through which certain substances can pass.

animal, cellulose, chloroplasts, fibrous, membrane, photosynthesis, plant

12 Starch, Sugar, Enzymes

Here's a bit of fun replicating what happens when we put certain foods in our mouths.

Test-tubes A and B both contain water and a length of partially permeable Visking tubing sealed at both ends. The tubing in A contains a starch suspension; the tubing in B contains starch suspension and saliva. Both test-tubes are kept at body temperature for 30 minutes. Samples from the water and samples from the suspension are then taken.

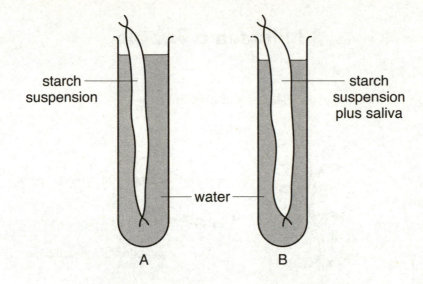

starch suspension

starch suspension plus saliva

water

A

B

How can you test a sample of liquid for starch?

How can you test a sample of liquid for reducing sugars?

Indicate in the table below where you'd expect to find starch or reducing sugars.

Water A	Solution in Visking A	Water B	Solution in Visking B

Answers on page 203

13 Plant in a Bubble

Here's a potted plant sealed in a transparent bag:

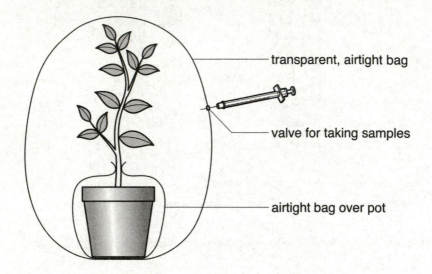

transparent, airtight bag

valve for taking samples

airtight bag over pot

Carbon dioxide concentration from the air in the bag is measured every hour. The plant is in direct sunlight for the first 3 hours, then placed in a dark cupboard for a further 3 hours. Over the first 3 hours, the carbon dioxide levels drop from 10 to 0 arbitrary units. Why?

Over the next 3 hours, the carbon dioxide levels rise again to 6 arbitrary units. Why?

Answers on page 204

14 Immune System

You know (don't you?) that white blood cells are important in our immune system. But try filling in the following sentence to resurrect your knowledge of how they work.

'As part of our immune system we have two main groups of ——— , lymphocytes and phagocytes. ——— are capable of ingesting or absorbing pathogens or toxins, and can also release an enzyme to destroy them. ——— ,on the other hand carry ——— to bind to and render harmless an ——— .'

antibodies, antigen, lymphocytes, phagocytes, white blood cells

15 Eye of the Tiger

Can you distinguish between predatory animals and their prey by observing some of their physical attributes? One look at a dog's teeth should give you an idea that dogs are naturally predatory creatures. Similarly, cows have teeth ideally suited for grinding plants, not murdering your adorable pets.

How about the configuration of an animal's eyes? If an animal has eyes on the front of its head, what does that suggest? Why is that configuration beneficial to it? And what about eyes on the side of the head – what sort of animal has those, and why?

Answers on page 204

CHEMISTRY

Atoms, molecules, elements, compounds. Acids, bases and salts. The Periodic Table. Boiling points and freezing points. Sublimation, condensation and evaporation. You remember at least some of that, don't you? That was all chemistry.

1	2	3	4	5	6	7	8	9	10	11	12	13	14	15	16	17	18
1 H Hydrogen 1.00794																	2 He Helium 4.003
3 Li Lithium 6.941	4 Be Beryllium 9.012182											5 B Boron 10.811	6 C Carbon 12.0107	7 N Nitrogen 14.00674	8 O Oxygen 15.9994	9 F Fluorine 18.9984032	10 Ne Neon 20.1797
11 Na Sodium 23	12 Mg Magnesium 24											13 Al Aluminium 26.981538	14 Si Silicon 28.0855	15 P Phosphorus 30.973761	16 S Sulphur 32.066	17 Cl Chlorine 35.4527	18 Ar Argon 39.948
19 K Potassium 39.0983	20 Ca Calcium 40.078	21 Sc Scandium 44.955910	22 Ti Titanium 47.867	23 V Vanadium 50.9415	24 Cr Chromium 51.9961	25 Mn Manganese 54.938049	26 Fe Iron 55.845	27 Co Cobalt 58.933200	28 Ni Nickel 58.6934	29 Cu Copper 63.546	30 Zn Zinc 65.39	31 Ga Gallium 69.723	32 Ge Germanium 72.61	33 As Arsenic 74.92160	34 Se Selenium 78.96	35 Br Bromine 79.904	36 Kr Krypton 83.80
37 Rb Rubidium 85.4678	38 Sr Strontium 87.62	39 Y Yttrium 88.90585	40 Zr Zirconium 91.224	41 Nb Niobium 92.90638	42 Mo Molybdenum 95.94	43 Tc Technetium (98)	44 Ru Ruthenium 101.07	45 Rh Rhodium 102.90550	46 Pd Palladium 106.42	47 Ag Silver 107.8682	48 Cd Cadmium 112.411	49 In Indium 114.818	50 Sn Tin 118.710	51 Sb Antimony 121.760	52 Te Tellurium 127.60	53 I Iodine 126.90447	54 Xe Xenon 131.29
55 Cs Cesium 132.90545	56 Ba Barium 137.327	57 La Lanthanum 138.9055	72 Hf Hafnium 178.49	73 Ta Tantalum 180.9479	74 W Tungsten 183.84	75 Re Rhenium 186.207	76 Os Osmium 190.23	77 Ir Iridium 192.217	78 Pt Platinum 195.078	79 Au Gold 196.96655	80 Hg Mercury 200.59	81 Tl Thallium 204.3833	82 Pb Lead 207.2	83 Bi Bismuth 208.98038	84 Po Polonium (209)	85 At Astatine (210)	86 Rn Radon (222)
87 Fr Francium (223)	88 Ra Radium (226)	89 Ac Actinium (227)	104 Rf Rutherfordium (267)	105 Db Dubnium (268)	106 Sg Seaborgium (271)	107 Bh Bohrium (272)	108 Hs Hassium (270)	109 Mt Meitnerium (276)	110 Ds Darmstadtium (281)	111 Rg Roentgenium (280)	112 Uub Ununbium (285)	113 Uut Ununtrium (284)	114 Uuq Ununquadium (289)	115 Uup Ununpentium (288)	116 Uuh Ununhexium (293)	117 Uus Ununseptium (294)	118 Uuo Ununoctium (294)

58 Ce Cerium 140.116	59 Pr Praseodymium 140.90765	60 Nd Neodymium 144.24	61 Pm Promethium (145)	62 Sm Samarium 150.36	63 Eu Europium 151.964	64 Gd Gadolinium 157.25	65 Tb Terbium 158.92534	66 Dy Dysprosium 162.50	67 Ho Holmium 164.93032	68 Er Erbium 167.26	69 Tm Thulium 168.93421	70 Yb Ytterbium 173.04	71 Lu Lutetium 174.967
90 Th Thorium 232.0381	91 Pa Protactinium 231.03588	92 U Uranium 238.0289	93 Np Neptunium (237)	94 Pu Plutonium (244)	95 Am Americium (243)	96 Cm Curium (247)	97 Bk Berkelium (247)	98 Cf Californium (251)	99 Es Einsteinium (252)	100 Fm Fermium (257)	101 Md Mendelevium (258)	102 No Nobelium (259)	103 Lr Lawrencium (262)

1 The Periodic Table

We all know what it looks like (but we've printed it on the previous page anyway); some of us may even have a vague idea of what it is about. So let's put that to the test, shall we?

Categorize the following chemical elements into their correct groups – alkali metals, halogens and noble gases:

caesium

fluorine

iodine

krypton

neon

potassium

2 Atomic Bonds

Casting your mind back to some fundamentals of chemistry – atoms, electrons and the desire for 'complete orbits' – you'll probably remember some key principles of sharing and exchanging electrons to form bonds.

What are covalent bonds and ionic bonds? Can you categorize the following molecules by the chemical bonds they involve?

Carbon dioxide, CO_2

Hydrogen, H_2

Potassium chloride, KCl

Sodium fluoride, NaF

Water, H_2O

Answers on page 205

3 It's All a Balancing Act

Did you do the chemical equations for respiration or photosynthesis at school? Remember a bunch of 6s and 12s? See if you can fill in the gaps to balance these equations. (Hint: sometimes you need only one of an item, so not all the gaps need to be filled.)

A. $- SnO_2 + - H_2 \rightarrow - Sn + - H_2O$

B. $- NaOH + - H_2SO_4 \rightarrow - Na_2SO_4 + - H_2O$

C. $- CBr_4 + - O_2 \rightarrow - CO_2 + - Br_2$

D. $- CO_2 + - H_2O \rightarrow - C_6H_{12}O_6 + - O_2$

4 Some Hydrocarbons

Can you line up the chemical formulae with the facts?

1. C_3H_6

2. CH_4

3. $C_5H_{10}O_4$

4. C_2H_4

A. The simplest alkane

B. The monomer which forms polyethene

C. An unsaturated hydrocarbon with three carbon atoms per molecule

D. Not a hydrocarbon!

5 Balloons

Four balloons are filled to equal volume with, respectively, helium, neon, argon and krypton gas. Each balloon is tied at one end to a separate long coil of string which freely unravels as the balloon rises. The coils of string are identical. The balloons are allowed to rise, and each comes to rest when the weight of the string it has lifted is equal to the up-thrust due to density differences inside and outside the balloon. In what order do the balloons sit, going from lowest to highest?

6 Ionic compounds

Here's a table with some ionic compounds – can you complete it?

Compound	Constituent Ions	Chemical Formula
Sodium Nitrate	NO_3^- , Na^+	
Aluminium Sulphate	Al^{3+} , SO_4^{2-}	
Barium Bromide	Ba^{2+} , Br^-	

7 Testing Your Reactions

Below is a diagram of lithium, sodium and potassium reacting with water. Can you match the letter of the beaker to the metal in it?

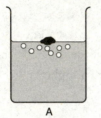
A

B

C

8 Name that Alkene!

Remember how to name your monomers? Name the alkene from its diagram. (If you don't remember what an alkene is, you're in good company – it's glossed over in many a syllabus. But even so, you probably learned the names.)

Answers on page 206

9 Fractional Distillation

Crude oil is packed with useful hydrocarbons, including alkanes. To separate them so that we can then turn them into even more useful hydrocarbons, we use a process called fractional distillation (heat the crude oil a lot and the compounds with lower boiling points will rise to the top of the mixture, so different fractions are physically separated).

Can you match the hydrocarbons listed below to their boiling points in the chamber on the right of the diagram?

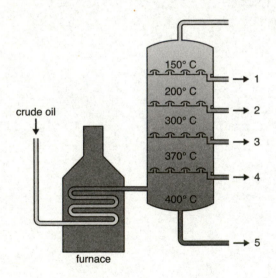

A.   Diesel oil

B.   Fuel oil

C.   Gasoline (petrol)

D.   Kerosene

E.   Lubricating oil, paraffin wax, asphalt

116

10 Cracking

Once we've got our hydrocarbons separated and we have some alkanes handy, we can make alkenes by a process called cracking. Make sense of this by filling in the gaps in these sentences, using the words given below (and using several of them more than once):

———— have some ———— between ————, meaning there is room for another ————, or for linking to further ————.

———— are hydrocarbons with only ————, whereas all ———— have ———— somewhere (otherwise they're not ————).

alkanes, alkenes, carbons, double bonds, hydrogen, single bonds, unsaturated hydrocarbons

And, once you've sorted that, give a reason why alkenes are useful, other than as fuel.

11 Sustainable Production of Alkenes

Crude oil, I'm sure you're aware, is a limited resource over which we're causing ourselves a lot of grief. But it doesn't have to be that way. We know from biology that yeast, water and sugar can be used to make ethanol. Let's look at a process for turning ethanol into ethene, which can then be used as a fuel, or made into a plastic like polyethene or PVC.

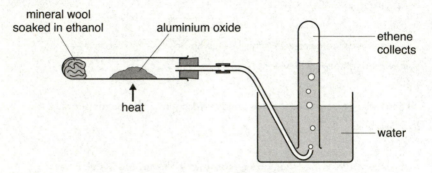

What is the purpose of the aluminium oxide here?

Can you complete this chemical equation for the process?

$$C_2H_5OH \xrightarrow{Al_2O_3} C_2H_4 + \underline{\hspace{3cm}}$$

12 Changes of State

Matter lives in different states depending on how much energy there is in the system. We're sometimes painfully aware of this when driving in winter. Can you remember the names for the changes of state? Try filling in this diagram with terms from the list below:

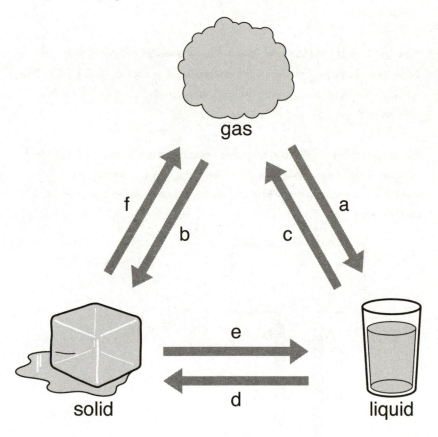

1. Sublimation
2. Evaporation
3. Freezing
4. Condensation
5. Deposition
6. Melting

Answers on page 208

13 Electrolysis

When an ionic compound is molten or in an aqueous solution, its ions are free to move. As a result the liquid can carry electrical current.

First of all, can you remember the names for negatively and positively charged ions?

Now let's look at what happens when we put a potential difference (voltage) across two electrodes and dunk them in a molten ionic compound (lead bromide – $PbBr_2$). On the diagram, name the electrodes labelled A and B: one is the cathode and one is the anode, but which is which?

As our current flows, solid lead begins to deposit at one electrode and bubbles of bromine gas start appearing at the other. Can you work out which way around this happens? (Hint, bromine forms Br^- negative ions and lead forms Pb^{2+} positive ions.)

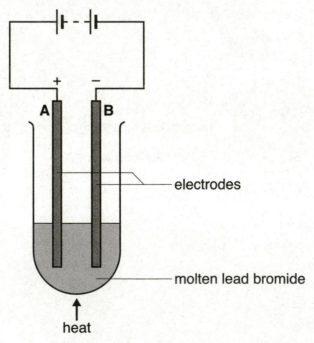

electrodes

molten lead bromide

heat

14 Ozone

Toxic as ozone (O_3) may be to us down here in the troposphere, it plays a hugely important role in protecting us from harmful UV rays up there in the stratosphere. Remember all the fuss about CFCs – chlorofluorocarbons – when we first started worrying about global warming? Let's take an example CFC to look at how it depletes our ozone layer.

CCl_3F or CFC-11, used in refrigeration, aerosols and foams, makes its way up to the stratosphere, where there's plenty of UV radiation to smash the molecules apart. Complete the following chemical equation for chlorine atoms being released from CCl_3F under the action of UV radiation:

$$CCl_3F \rightarrow \text{_____} + Cl$$

Moving on from this, complete another equation to show what this free chlorine atom can now do to an ozone molecule:

$$Cl + O_3 \rightarrow O_2 + \text{_____}$$

So we've lost an ozone molecule. But it gets worse: there are plenty of lone oxygen atoms around, and they can liberate the chlorine from the chlorine compound produced in the previous equation to break yet more ozone molecules! Complete this to show how the chlorine atom is re-liberated:

$$\text{_____} + O \rightarrow O_2 + Cl$$

Answers on page 208

15 Catalytic Converters

The presence of catalysts in a car's exhaust system can significantly reduce the amount of harmful gases released into the atmosphere.

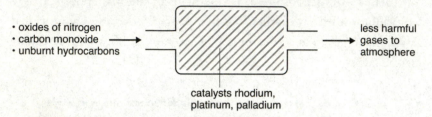

• oxides of nitrogen
• carbon monoxide
• unburnt hydrocarbons

less harmful gases to atmosphere

catalysts rhodium, platinum, palladium

Oxides of nitrogen form an example. Rhodium catalyses the decomposition of nitric oxide (which reacts with ozone) like so:

$$2NO \rightarrow N_2 + O_2$$

Can you produce equations to show how in a catalytic converter:

A.   Carbon monoxide is oxidized to carbon dioxide

B.   An unburnt hydrocarbon, C_3H_8, is oxidized to carbon dioxide and water.

PHYSICS

'The branch of science concerned with the properties of matter and energy and the relationships between them,' says the dictionary. It's about waves and reflections and electric currents and all those laws to do with gases. And to be honest, that's about all I know. I had help with this bit.

1 Half-Life

If you're going to talk about radioactive isotopes with that cute environmental activist you met at the market, you'd better get back up to speed on your understanding of these materials.

Plutonium has a half-life of 24,000 years. How many years will it take for a sample of plutonium to become 12.5% as active as it is today?

2 Electromagnetic Spectrum

The uses of electromagnetic radiation seem to have no end – from letting us see to mobile communication, studying distant galaxies, warming mini-pizzas, operating speed cameras and controlling our television sets. Our daily lives involve electromagnetic radiation so much that it would be just plain rude not to keep on familiar terms with this beauty of nature. Can you organize these 'types' (it's all the same stuff, just with different names for different frequency ranges) of EM radiation, in ascending order of frequency?

Answers on page 209

AM radio waves

Gamma rays

Infra-red

Microwaves

Ultraviolet light

Visible blue light

Visible green light

Visible red light

X-rays

3 The Line of Least Resistance

Have a look at this circuit.

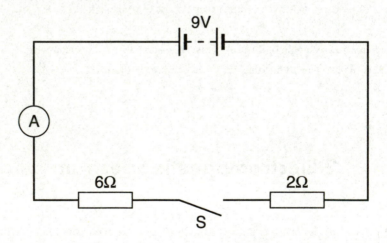

1.   What's the reading on the ammeter A while the switch S is open?
2.   What's the reading on A when S is closed?
3.   What's the potential difference across the 6 ohm resistor when S is closed?
4.   What's the potential difference across the 2 ohm resistor when S is closed?

4 A Tough One for Left-handers

Here's a diagram of an electric motor in action.

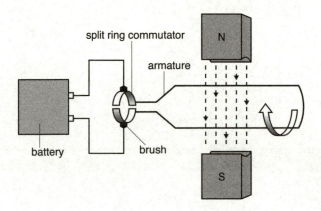

split ring commutator

armature

N

S

battery

brush

Use the right-hand rule to determine which is the positive terminal of the battery.

5 Waves

OK, do you remember this equation:

$v = f\,\lambda$

What do the letters mean?

If I play a note of wavelength 25cm on my 1980s keyboard, knowing that the speed of sound is 340ms^{-1} in air, what is the frequency of the note?

If the speed of light is 3×10^8ms^{-1}, what wavelength has a microwave of frequency 2,450MHz?

Answers on page 210–11

6 Vanity

Mirror, mirror . . .

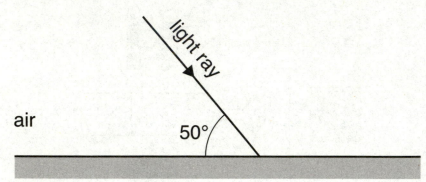

OK, that's enough admiring ourselves. Let's do some work. What is the angle of incidence of the light ray hitting the mirror in the diagram above? What is its angle of reflection as it bounces off the mirror?

7 Water Waves

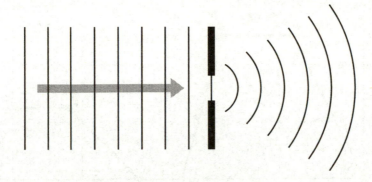

Take a look at what happens to the crest of the water waves in the diagram above as they hit a wall with a gap in it. What is this effect of the waves curving as they cross the boundary called?

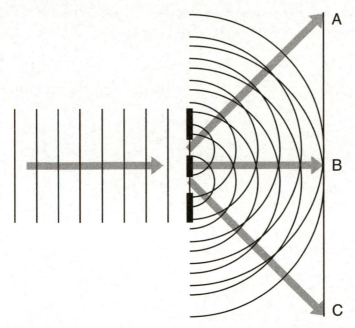

Now if we send the crests of the waves at a wall with 2 slits in it, the effect happens at each hole and, as we can see, the waves interfere at the other side of the wall. What occurs along the lines A, B and C?

Answers on page 211

8 A Race Against Time

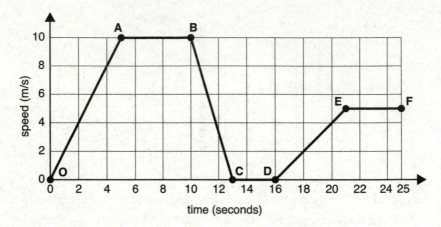

The above graph shows the speed of a motorbike against time as it makes its way to the pet shop. How far does the motorbike travel between O and F?

Answers on page 212

9 Hooke's Law

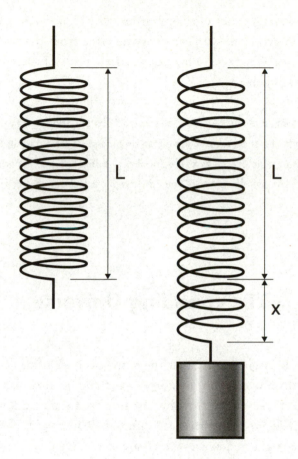

Here you see a light spring (meaning I consider it to have no weight) hanging with no weight attached to the end, and another one with a weight attached. If x=1cm when I attach a weight of 200g mass to the spring hanging at rest, what is x when I attach a further 200g? What about if I attach a total of 500g?

10 Potential Energy and Efficiency

There are several types of potential energy. That which strikes fear into our hearts when we peer over the edge from the top of a tall building is called gravitational potential energy and that is what we are looking at here.

I have a motorized pulley system which lifts a 250kg lion (don't worry, it's a comfortable harness) 6 metres in the air (to be placed on a boat for its trip to freedom). The system uses 5kW of electrical power and takes 8 seconds to perform the lift. How efficient is it? You can take the acceleration due to gravity to be 9.8ms^{-1}.

11 Expanding Universe

You've probably been told that the universe is expanding. How do we know this? To jog your memory, when certain chemical reactions occur, like those which fuel the burning of distant stars, light rays of very particular frequencies are emitted. When we look at distant stars, we see light frequencies which are almost what we'd expect, but a touch lower. This effect is called Doppler shift (or red shift in this specific test, since the colours we see are little redder than we'd expect).

So, having reminded yourself of all that, if a siren sounds at 440Hz on a car driving away from you at 20ms^{-1}, what frequency do you hear? (Hint: sound travels at 340ms^{-1} in air, and you could work out how far the car has travelled in the time between peaks in the 400Hz sound wave.)

12 Newton's Second Law

First of all, do you know what Newton's Second Law says? Good. Now use it to solve this problem:

If there are 5 hippies in a camper-van of total mass (including passengers) 2000kg, accelerating at 2ms^{-2} against combined resistances of 150N, what forward force is the engine applying to the vehicle?

13 Heat Transfer

Can you recall the three different types of heat transfer? And do you remember which is which?

A.   What name is used for the process of heating a fluid in a container (like air in a room) by use of a single heat source, causing heat currents in the fluid to distribute the energy throughout the container?

B.   What name is used for the transmission of heat from a glowing bar heater such as those found on masts in smoking areas outside pubs?

C.   What name is used for the transmission of heat through a solid like a metal spoon left in a heating pan (ouch!)?

Answers on page 213

14 Gas Laws

You may remember Boyle's Law, Charles' Law and the like. Well, add them to Gay-Lussac's Law and you have the Combined Gas Law, which states that

$$\frac{pV}{T} = k$$

where k is a constant, and p, V and T are pressure, volume and temperature respectively.

Let's have a little gas workout and see how changing one parameter can affect the others.

I have a cylinder with a plunger (like a big syringe) to allow volume changes. This cylinder contains gas at a pressure of $4Nm^{-2}$, temperature 300K and volume $0.5m^3$.

A.   What is the pressure inside the cylinder if I push the plunger in to halve the volume, somehow keeping the temperature the same?

B.   What happens to the pressure if instead I maintain the volume while cooling the gas to $\frac{1}{3}$ of its original temperature (assuming the gas remains as a gas)?

C.   Or, maintaining the volume, what temperature increase would cause the pressure to increase by a factor of 1.5?

15 Gravity

Do you remember those equations for a body under constant acceleration? Gravity provides (to a very good approximation) constant acceleration on a falling marble. Let's see what you can do.

A.   If I tilt a table and allow my marble to roll (from rest) along the top for 2 seconds at a constant acceleration of $3ms^{-2}$, how fast does the marble get?

B.   If I drop my marble from a height of 6m, how long does it take to hit the ground?

16 Drag Race

Who can dress–up like a member of the opposite sex quickest? No.

Soraya has built a drag racer (with just one gear) that accelerates at precisely $5ms^{-2}$. If it does this over a 400m race, what speed does it reach as it crosses the finish line?

17 Thirsty Work

If I apply a constant force of 60N to a huge crate of beer as I push it along a rough horizontal surface (like my neighbour's lawn), how much work have I done against friction after pushing it for 20 metres?

18 Dogs and their Toys

My dog is chasing a tennis ball rolling along flat wet sand. The ball is 10m ahead of him, he is running at a constant speed of $10ms^{-1}$ and the ball is rolling at $15ms^{-1}$ and decelerating due to friction at a rate of $0.5ms^{-2}$. How long before the dog gets the ball? What speed is the ball doing when he catches it?

19 Specific Heat Capacity

Even if you don't remember this term, you may remember being asked how much energy it takes to heat 1kg of water by 1°C. That's the specific heat capacity of water, and it's about 4186 $Jkg^{-1}K^{-1}$.

OK, I want to fill my 330ml coffee mug with 300ml of boiling water. I put 300ml of water at 15°C into my 94% efficient 3kW kettle. How long does it take to get the boiling water I want? (Assume that 1L of water has a mass of 1kg.)

7 GENERAL STUDIES

This was the catch-all subject that allowed you to keep up with music, art, religious studies and the classics even if there wasn't an exam at the end of it. This chapter follows the same miscellaneous pattern – with the difference that there is a test on every page.

1 Musical Instructions

. . . are usually given in Italian. Match these words to their meaning when applied to a piece of music.

1. Allegro
2. Andante
3. Cantabile
4. Diminuendo
5. Largo
6. Pianissimo
7. Presto
8. Scherzo
9. Staccato
10. Vivace

A. At a walking pace
B. Cheerful
C. Detached, not held down
D. Growing quieter
E. Lively
F. Playful
G. Quick
H. As if it were being sung
I. Slow
J. Very quiet

Answers on page 216

2 Papal Bull

Which of the following is not the name of a Pope?

Adrian, Bernardo, Celestine, Conon, Eugene, Felix, Lando, Martin, Stephen, Sylvester, Valentine

3 Roman Numerals

Write the following years in Roman numerals:

1. 1066
2. 1415
3. 1588
4. 1666
5. 1776
6. 1865
7. 1945
8. 2001

Answers on page 216

4 Deus ex Machina

Among the Roman gods there were a number who had Greek equivalents. Match them up, and link them to their areas of expertise.

ROMAN

1. Ceres
2. Diana
3. Juno
4. Jupiter
5. Mars
6. Mercury
7. Minerva
8. Neptune
9. Venus
10. Vulcan

GREEK

A. Aphrodite
B. Ares
C. Artemis
D. Athena
E. Demeter
F. Hephaestus
G. Hera
H. Hermes
I. Poseidon
J. Zeus

FUNCTION/RESPONSIBILITY

I. Crops and the harvest
II. Father of the gods
III. Fire
IV. Hunting

Answers on page 217

V. Love

VI. Marriage

VII. Messenger of the gods

VIII. The sea

IX. War

X. Wisdom

5 The Muses

Still in Greek mythology, there were nine Muses, daughters of Zeus, who lived on Mount Parnassus and inspired different fields of music, the arts and science. Can you match each Muse to her area of expertise?

1. Calliope

2. Clio

3. Erato

4. Euterpe

5. Melpomene

6. Polymnia

7. Terpsichore

8. Thalia

9. Urania

A. Astronomy

B. Comedy

C. Dance

D. Epic or heroic poetry

E. History

F. Love poetry

G. Music and lyric poetry

H. Sacred song

I. Tragedy

Answers on page 217

6 Heroes and Heroines of Antiquity

Match these mythical and legendary figures to their exploits:

1. Achilles
2. Jason
3. Medea
4. Medusa
5. Oedipus
6. Pandora
7. Paris
8. Perseus
9. Prometheus
10. Theseus

A. Abducted Helen of Troy, thus sparking off the Trojan War
B. Found the golden fleece
C. Had serpents in her hair and turned anyone who looked at her to stone
D. Killed a monster called the Minotaur, which lived in the Labyrinth in Crete
E. Killed his father, married his mother, ending up tearing his own eyes out
F. Murdered her own children to be revenged on her unfaithful husband
G. Rescued Andromeda, who was chained to a rock and about to be eaten by a sea serpent
H. Stole fire from heaven and was punished by being chained to a rock where an eagle pecked constantly at his liver
I. Was the greatest Greek warrior in the Trojan War, invincible unless you caught him in a particular spot
J. Was the first woman on earth and owned a box she wasn't supposed to open

Answers on page 218

7 A Prophet in His Own Country

Test your biblical knowledge: the latter part of the Old Testament consists almost entirely of books named after prophets. Three of these are termed the 'major' prophets' and thirteen the 'minor' ones.

So:

1.   How many of them can you name?
2.   How close can you get to the right order? And
3.   What is the one book in the last seventeen of the Old Testament that isn't simply named after a prophet?

8 Biblical Quotations

Many, many expressions from the Bible have passed into everyday use. Fill in the missing words from the list given. In the example where more than one word is missing, it is (more or less) the same word repeated, and it may help to realise that the quotations are given in alphabetical order.

1.   Am I my ——'s keeper?
2.   Blessed are the ——, for they shall inherit the earth
3.   Consider the —— of the field, how they grow; they toil not, neither do they spin
4.   I am escaped with the —— of my teeth
5.   It is easier for a —— to go through the eye of a needle, than for a rich man to enter the kingdom of God
6.   Man is born unto trouble, as the —— fly upward
7.   Suffer the little —— to come unto me and forbid them not

Answers on page 218–19

8. To every thing there is a —, and a time to every purpose under the heaven

9. — of —s, saith the Preacher, — of —s, all is —

10. Who can find a virtuous woman? For her price is far above —

A. Brother

B. Camel

C. Children

D. Lilies

E. Meek

F. Rubies

G. Season

H. Skin

I. Sparks

J. Vanity (and vanities)

9 The New Testament

To which of these peoples did Saint Paul *not* write a letter (or 'epistle')?

1. Alexandrians

2. Colossians

3. Corinthians

4. Ephesians

5. Galatians

6. Romans

7. Thessalonians

. . . and which of these wasn't one of the original twelve disciples?

A. Andrew

B. Bartholomew

C. James

142

D. Matthew

E. Philip

F. Timothy

Finally – and this is an Old Testament question – who are the only two women to have books of the Bible named after them?

10 The Seven Deadly Sins

Simple question – can you name them? (No points for saying, 'No', even though it might be an accurate answer.)

Less well known, perhaps, are the Seven Virtues, sometimes called the Catholic Virtues. Three of these are traditionally described as the theological or Christian virtues, the other four as the cardinal virtues. Can you name them?

11 Wonders Will Never Cease

If the Seven Wonders of the Ancient World were still with us today, two of them would be in Egypt, one in mainland Greece and one on a Greek island, two in Turkey and one in Iraq. Can you name them and sort them out?

Answers on page 219

12 Hindu Gods

The Hindus have a whole pantheon of gods with colourful (both literally and figuratively) attributes. Can you sort out the two lists?

1. Krishna
2. Kali
3. Lakshmi
4. Durga
5. Shiva
6. Hanuman
7. Vishnu
8. Ganesh

144

A.   A fierce warrior goddess, often with eight or ten arms, riding a tiger.

B.   The destroyer of the world, often depicted holding a trident and dancing.

C.   The elephant god – a human body with an elephant's head.

D.   The goddess of destruction, depicted with long ragged hair and fangs or tusks.

E.   The goddess of light, beauty and good fortune. Depicted as a beautiful woman, often standing or seated on a lotus flower.

F.   The monkey god, seen as the ideal faithful servant.

G.   The preserver of creation, he never sleeps and is usually depicted with four arms and holding a mace.

H.   The Supreme Being, but also the god of human desires and failings. Sometimes depicted as a young boy with a flute; when shown as an older man he has a dark, often blue, face.

13 Composers

Match the first name to the surname and then to the nationality:

1.   Antonín
2.   Arnold
3.   Edvard
4.   Franz
5.   Frédéric
6.   Gustav
7.   Jean
8.   Johannes
9.   Maurice
10.   Sergei

A.   Brahms
B.   Chopin
C.   Dvořák

Answers on page 220–1

D. Grieg

E. Holst

F. Liszt

G. Rachmaninoff

H. Ravel

I. Schoenberg

J. Sibelius

I. Austrian

II. British

III. Czech

IV. Finnish

V. French

VI. German

VII. Hungarian

VIII. Norwegian

IX. Polish

X. Russian

Answers on page 221

14 Musical notes

Can you match the name to the note?

Breve

Semibreve or whole note

Minim or half note

Crotchet or quarter note

Quaver or eighth note

Semiquaver or sixteenth note

Demisemiquaver or thirty-second note and

Hemidemisemiquaver or sixty-fourth note

15 Musical forms

Anyone who listens to classical music will probably be familiar with the terms listed below. But, be honest, do you have any idea what they mean? Can you match the form to the definition?

1. Cantata
2. Chamber music
3. Concerto
4. Fugue
5. Oratorio
6. Prelude
7. Rondo

Answers on page 221

8. Sonata

9. Symphony

10. Toccata

A. A form of composition, usually instrumental, in which one section recurs intermittently

B. A large-scale work for full orchestra, usually in four movements

C. A musical setting of a usually religious subject, for solo singers, choir and orchestra

D. A work for a number of parts or voices, in which each enters in turn, imitating the previous one

E. A work for a solo instrument backed by an orchestra

F. A work for solo piano or piano and one other instrument

G. A work that may be self-contained but is usually designed to precede something else, such as a fugue

H. A work, usually for a keyboard instrument, played quickly and with lots of scope for showing off the performer's skill

I. Music written for a small number of instruments, with no soloist. Often a string quartet.

J. Various sorts of work designed to be sung, from a succession of arias to a mini-oratorio

16 Great Artists, Great Works

Link these artists to their works. I've given all the titles in English, though two at least may be more familiar in their original language.

1. Sandro Botticelli
2. John Constable
3. Paul Gauguin
4. Vincent van Gogh
5. Edouard Manet
6. Michelangelo Buonarotti
7. Claude Monet
8. Auguste Rodin
9. Diego Velázquez
10. Leonardo da Vinci

A. The Birth of Venus
B. David
C. The Haywain
D. Luncheon on the Grass
E. The Maids of Honour
F. Starry Night
G. Two Tahitian Women
H. The Thinker
I. The Virgin of the Rocks
J. Water Lilies

For a few bonus points, list the artists in chronological order of their birth.

Answers on page 222

ANSWERS

ENGLISH LANGUAGE ANSWERS

1 Parts of Speech

NOUNS

1. 1. years, father, advice
2. 2. scene, vault, schoolroom
3. 3. Paris, dark, evening, luxury, meditation, meerschaum. Note that *dark* can, of course, be an adjective ('It was a dark and stormy night') but is here used as a noun, a synonym for 'nightfall'.

PRONOUNS

1. me
2. there are none
3. I

ADJECTIVES

1. younger, vulnerable, some
2. plain, bare, monotonous
3. gusty, twofold

2 Parts of Speech 2

VERBS

1. is, do, have done
2. were
3. had been settled

ADVERBS

1. far, far, ever
2. particularly, admirably
3. long. Again, this word is often used as an adjective, but here it is the equivalent of 'for a long time'.

PREPOSITIONS

1. none
2. to
3. of, in

3 Parts of Speech 3

CONJUNCTIONS

and, and, but, so

DETERMINERS

his, the, the, my, a

INTERJECTIONS

ahem

4 Keep It Simple

1A. Desipient = foolish

2G. Effulgent = shining brightly

3F. Inchoate = rudimentary, immature

4E. Lachrymose = prone to weeping

5C. Lubricious = lewd

6H. Meretricious = superficially attractive, insincere

7D. Minutious = nit-picking (it's connected with *minutiae*)

8I. Nugatory = trifling, of little importance

9J. Otiose = useless, serving no purpose

10B. Piligerous = hairy

5 Keep It Simple 2

1E. Bedizen = decorate in a gaudy way

2J. Beshrew = wish harm on, curse

3B. Confabulate = chat or confer with

4I. Contrist = sadden

5A. Eructate = burp

6G. Lucubrate = explain or amplify in a scholarly way

7C. Masticate = chew

8D. Obnubilate = darken, obscure

9F. Periclitate = endanger

10H. Tergiversate = forsake, abandon (literally to turn your back on)

6 Get it Right

1. This is correct – if you told her that her scarf complemented her dress you would be paying her a *compliment*.

2. Change to *uninterested*: if you are disinterested in reality TV it means you have an open mind about who wins.

3. You mean *gregarious*, friendly, enjoying meeting new people. Egregious means standing out from the crowd.

4. *Enormousness* is a mouthful, so better avoided, but it is what you mean. The vastness of his fortune is also correct. Enormity means dreadfulness, as in 'He realized the enormity of his crime.'

5. This is correct. The common mistake is to say *founder*, which is what a sinking ship or a failing project does.

6. You mean *fortunate*, because it was a piece of good luck. Fortuitous means that it happened by chance, but may have been fortunate or unfortunate.

7. Fulsome means that the praise was overdone, insincere. Assuming the English teacher meant what she said, she might have been enthusiastic or generous in her praise.

8. This is correct. In this sentence, the speaker *infers* that whoever she is speaking to dislikes her mother, because that is what he has *implied*.

9. A simple spelling mistake. *To loathe* means to hate; what is wanted here is *loath* or *loth*.

10. You mean *straitened*, as in a *strait* (a narrow body of water) or a *straitjacket*.

7 Where Do They All Come From?

1. *Algebra – modern Iran*: the term to describe using letters to represent numbers in equations and the like was coined by a ninth-century Persian mathematician and comes from the Arabic for 'reunion'.

2. *Cenotaph – France*: the word ultimately derives from the Greek for 'empty tomb' but it entered the English language via French in the early seventeenth century.

3. *Chocolate – Mexico*: one of the many foodstuffs discovered by the Spanish *conquistadores* when they invaded Mexico in the sixteenth century and brought back by them to Europe. We owe them avocados, chillies and tomatoes too.

4. *Compound – Malaysia*: from the Malay *kampong*, meaning 'enclosure, village, cluster of buildings'. All the other meanings of compound, such as a chemical compound or a compound noun, derive from this.

5. *Diva – Italy*: the Italian for 'goddess' has come to mean the leading lady of an opera or any celebrated female singer, particularly one who behaves in a demanding and high-handed manner.

6. *Macho – Spain*: *macho* is the everyday Spanish word for 'male', used in English to mean aggressively masculine.

7. *Robot – Czech Republic*: coined by the Czech author Karel Capek in his play *R.U.R.*, written in 1920. *R.U.R.* stands for *Rossum's Universal Robots*, and the play is about artificial people who have been created in order to do the work of humans but who, being able to think for themselves, rebel and destroy the human race. The word derives from the Czech for 'drudgery'.

8. *Shampoo – India*: this comes from the Hindi for 'to press' and originally meant to give a relaxing massage. From there it developed first into the act of massaging the scalp and thence of washing the hair, and finally into the soapy stuff itself.

9. *Typhoon – China*: from the Cantonese for 'big wind'.

10. *Ukulele – Hawaii*: Portuguese immigrants to Hawaii in the nineteenth century took a small guitar with them; the Hawaiians adopted it and popularized it. Their name for it means 'jumping flea', apparently because of the way the player's fingers leap about on the fret board.

8 Which Is Which?

1. *Broach, brooch.* The first means to enter on a subject, the second is a piece of jewellery.
2. *Canvass;* a *canvas* is something an artist paints on, or that a tent is made of.
3. *Censured, censored: censured* means condemned or criticized; *to censor* is to cut out the naughty bits.
4. *Discreet. Discrete* means separate, self-contained.
5. *Forgo. Forego* isn't used very often, but it means to go before.
6. *Formally. Formerly* means at an earlier time.
7. *Hordes.* A *hoard* is something that is stored away, like a miser's gold.
8. *Pore. Pour* is what you do when you add milk to cereal.
9. *Principal* (= head teacher, main person), *principle* (= standard of conduct or belief).
10. *Rein. Reign* is what monarchs do.

9 Same Old, Same Old

1 & 7. Abreast, conversant
2 & 5. Acerbic, biting
3 & 18. Amorphous, shapeless
4 & 8. Benighted, desolate
6 & 13. Candid, frank
9 & 19. Desultory, spasmodic
10 & 16. Devastated, ravaged
11 & 20. Duplicitous, wily
12 & 17. Formidable, redoubtable
14 & 15. Humane, magnanimous

10 Opposites Attract

1 & 14. Assertive, obsequious
2 & 8. Biased, dispassionate
3 & 20. Blatant, unobtrusive
4 & 18. Congenial, repugnant
5 & 15. Contemporary, obsolete
6 & 11. Devious, guileless
7 & 16. Diaphanous, opaque

Answers on page xxx

9 & 19. Egotistical, selfless

10 & 17. Generous, parsimonious

12 & 13. Lucid, obscure

11 Spelling

The wrong ones and their correct spellings are:

1.   Allegedly

3.   Besiege

5.   Conference

7.   Delicatessen

8.   Deplorable

10. Fulfilment

12. Idiosyncrasy

13. Inoculate

14. Mantelpiece

18. Rigorous

12 Here Are the Answers; Now What's the Question?

1.   Conceit

2.   Detention

3.   Elocution

4.   Emancipation

5.   Genius

6.   Hypochondria

7.   Nostalgia

8.   Pachyderm

9.   Scrutiny

10. Tassel

13 A Question of Grammar

1.   *Yourself* is an emphatic pronoun and there is no need for emphasis here: 'I'll be able to send the paperwork to *you*' says exactly the same thing. If the speaker then went on to say, 'You must fill in the form *yourself* (i.e. not get anyone else to do it)', that would be a sensible use of the emphatic pronoun.

2.   These two clauses are not dependent on each other, so the comma between them is incorrect. If you said, 'I don't want to go to work today, so I'm going to phone in sick', the comma would be right, because that little word *so* turns the second part of the sentence into a subordinate clause. As it is, the two clauses have equal weight. Separating them by a semi-colon, a colon or a dash would be fine, as would inserting a full stop and making them two sentences. In other words, almost anything *except* a comma would be OK.

3.   *Only* should go next to the word it qualifies, which is *one: we drank only one beer* is correct. As it stands, the sentence says we only *drank* the beer, as opposed to, say, pouring it over someone's head.

4.   Grammatically, this sentence says that the skirt was dancing with Michael. This is what is called a misrelated participle or a dangling modifier. Rephrase as either 'As I danced with Michael, my skirt swirled around my ankles' or 'Dancing with Michael, I felt my skirt swirling around my ankles.'

5.   The words that follow *either* and *or* should be the same parts of speech or have the same construction. Thus either *Either you can apologise right now or you can go to bed without any supper* or *You can either apologise right now or go to bed without any supper* would be correct.

6.   The part that is wrong is *my husband and I. I* is the subject form of the pronoun; after a preposition you need the object form (in this case *me*). So I am sending something from *my husband and me*. If in doubt about this sort of construction, put a mental bracket round 'my husband and'. *I am sending a donation from I* is clearly wrong; so is *from my husband and I.*

7.   This is the distinction between *can* and *may*: of course you *can* ask me a favour, in the sense that you are capable of it. What you mean is *may I ask*, that is, do I have your permission to?

8.   *Who* is the form to use when it is the subject of a sentence. In this case you need the object: *the guide whom I spoke to* or *the guide to whom I spoke*. In informal speech you could leave it out altogether: *the guide I spoke to.*

9.   *Youngest* is a superlative and is used when comparing three or more objects

or people. As there are only two sisters, you need the comparative: Laura is the *younger*.

10. This is a tautology, pleonasm or redundancy: saying the same thing twice. If you said something originated for the second time, that would be nonsense; therefore it is unnecessary to say that it originated for the first time. The sense of *first* is implicit in the word *originated*.

14 Apostrophes? Who know's?

The basic rules for using apostrophes are surprisingly straightforward. An apostrophe indicates possession, or it shows that a letter or letters have been missed out. Also, it's important to remember not to use an apostrophe in possessive pronouns such as *hers* or *theirs*. So:

1. I *don't* want you to use my car. Why *can't* you use *yours*?
   Note the lack of apostrophe in *yours*. It's a possessive pronoun, standing for *your car*.

2. *Hers* are the only children I like. Everyone *else's* babies look like stewed prunes. Again, *hers* is a possessive pronoun – no apostrophe.

3. Is that *someone's* idea of a joke? I certainly *don't* think *it's* funny.

4. The river rises in the mountains and flows very quickly for its first few miles. No apostrophes: there isn't one in *its* when it is a possessive pronoun.

5. The *ladies'* cloakroom is upstairs; the *men's* is next to the *porter's* lodge. The apostrophe indicating possession goes after the s in a plural ending in s (as in *ladies*), but before the s when the plural does not end in s (as in *men*). *Porter's* indicates that there is only one porter; if there were more it would be *porters'*.

6. You can always recognize actresses, even the unknown ones: theirs are the voices you can hear across a crowded room.
   No apostrophes needed: *theirs* is another possessive pronoun.

7. The price of all shoes has been reduced in this *week's* sale.

8. *We'll* have to leave soon: *it's* nearly midnight.
   Here *we'll* is short for *we shall* and *it's* is short for *it is*, so both need apostrophes.

9. There are some very pretty *girls'* clothes in the shops. *It's* much harder to buy presents for boys.

As in question 5, *girls* is a possessive plural ending in s, so the apostrophe goes after the s; *it's* is short for *it is*.

10. *Everyone's* talking about the *president's* promises.

 Again, we're assuming there is only one president: if there were more it would be *presidents'*.

15 Collective Nouns

1H. A bevy of partridges (also a covey of partridges)

2D. A charm of goldfinches

3A. An intrusion of cockroaches

4F. A kindle of kittens

5G. A labour of moles

6B. A murder of crows

7I. A prickle of porcupines

8E. A swarm of jellyfish

9J. A shiver of sharks

10C. A tower of giraffes

16 Why Do We Say . . . ?

1D. To be in good working order a car's engine needs to 'fire on all cylinders' – hence the metaphor of a person or project being up, running and at its brightest and best.

2I. Hit the ground running comes from the idea that you are running away from someone, leaping off a train (the way they did in old films) and dashing off into the undergrowth, rather than falling over and lying in a crumpled heap to get your breath back. If you do this in a job context, you are fully functioning from day one, without the need for training or any other form of hand-holding.

3J. Having a safe pair of hands means you are likely to catch anything that is coming your way.

4G. Any outfielder in baseball is likely to be less involved in the action than an infielder, so something coming 'out of left field' may be unexpected or wacky. Why left rather than right? Probably because of the age-old prejudice that left is by definition just that little bit weird.

5H. In surveying, the benchmark was a fixed point into which a bench or bracket was inserted, enabling the surveyor to calculate the height and position of other points and another surveyor, coming along later, to insert his own bench in exactly the same place and start his calculations from the same premise. The same concept applies when you use the word metaphorically.

6E. The 'big picture' was the main feature in the cinema in the days when you got two movies for the price of one: the other would be the less starry, lower-budget 'B movie'.

7B. From the oil trade – a pipeline is simply a long pipe used to transport oil, natural gas, etc. over long distances. So something that is 'in the pipeline' is under way but hasn't arrived yet.

8A. The origins of this idiom may be literal (if you'd murdered someone and stashed the body away, you might end up decades later with a skeleton in the cupboard that you didn't want anyone to discover); or they may come from the early study of anatomy. Before dissecting a body for the purposes of medical research became legal in the 1830s, it was hard for a doctor anxious to improve his knowledge to get hold of enough corpses – hence the thriving trade in grave-robbing described in Charles Dickens's *A Tale of Two Cities*, to name but one. But it had to be done in great secrecy, so again the doctor, when he had finished his dissection, may have ended up with a skeleton in his cupboard.

9C. The jockey who is confident of victory doesn't need to whip his horse or jerk the reins.

10F. In the early days of boxing, the 'ring' was a patch of ground in the open air. A line – the scratch – was drawn across it to indicate where both boxers had to stand at the start of the match. Once one was knocked down, he was allowed thirty seconds to get his breath back, but then had to come 'up to the scratch' again and carry on. If he didn't, of course, he had lost.

17 Figures of Speech

1F. Alliteration involves a number of words beginning with the same sound.

2I. Euphemism is a way of avoiding saying something unpleasant, in this case 'to die'.

3B. Hyperbole is deliberate overstatement. You don't really thank someone a thousand times; you probably do it twice at the most.

4A. Litotes is the opposite of hyperbole – deliberate understatement.

5C. Actually, all the world *isn't* a stage. With a metaphor, you're just saying this for effect.

6J. Metonymy means using the name of one thing to represent an attribute of it or something with which it is associated. 'Washington' in this sense doesn't mean the entire city, it means the political entity associated with it. Similarly 'Wall Street' and 'the City' refer not to the literal streets and buildings but to the financial sectors based there.

7G. Onomatopoeia is using words to replicate the sound they are trying to convey.

8E. An oxymoron is an apparent contradiction, a juxtaposing of two words that don't normally go together.

9H. Personification means giving an object – in this case autumn, in Keats's ode – the attributes of a human being.

10D. The words *as* or *like* are the giveaway when it comes to similes. With a metaphor you say something *is* something else; a simile merely *compares*.

ENGLISH LITERATURE ANSWERS

1 Classic Heroines

1D. Dorothea Brooke, *Middlemarch*, George Eliot

2J. Catherine Earnshaw, *Wuthering Heights*, Emily Brontë

3F. Anne Elliot, *Persuasion*, Austen

4G. Lucie Manette, *A Tale of Two Cities*, Dickens

5E. Catherine Morland, *Northanger Abbey*, Austen

6C. Fanny Price, *Mansfield Park*, Austen

7H. Becky Sharp, *Vanity Fair*, Thackeray

8I. Lucy Snowe, *Villette*, Charlotte Bronte

9A. Esther Summerson, *Bleak House*, Dickens

10B. Agnes Wickfield, *David Copperfield*, Dickens

2 More Recent 'Classics'

1E. Ralph, Jack and Piggy, *Lord of the Flies*, William Golding

2H. Charles Arrowby, *The Sea, the Sea*, Iris Murdoch

3A. Pinkie Brown, *Brighton Rock*, Graham Greene

4J. Gudrun and Ursula Brangwen, *Women in Love*, D. H. Lawrence

5C. Holden Caulfield, *The Catcher in the Rye*, J. D. Salinger

6F. Jim Dixon, *Lucky Jim*, Kingsley Amis

7I. Scout and Jem Finch, *To Kill a Mockingbird*, Harper Lee

8D. Daphne Manners and Hari Kumar, *The Jewel in the Crown*, Paul Scott

9G. George Milton and Lennie Small, *Of Mice and Men*, John Steinbeck

10B. Captain Yossarian and Major Major, *Catch-22*, Joseph Heller

Supplementary answer: William Golding. He won the Booker for *Rites of Passage* in 1980 and was awarded the Nobel Prize in 1983.

3 Pick a Colour

1. *The Amber Spyglass*, Philip Pullman

2. *Black Beauty*, Anna Sewell

3. *The Blue Cross* (about the priest/detective Father Brown), G. K. Chesterton

4. *The Golden Notebook*, Doris Lessing

5. *Anne of Green Gables*, L. M. Montgomery

6. *A Clockwork Orange*, Anthony Burgess

7. *The Color Purple*, Alice Walker

8. *The Red-Headed League*, Arthur Conan Doyle

9. *The Scarlet Letter*, Nathaniel Hawthorne

10. *White Fang*, Jack London

4 Pick a Number

1. *A Tale of Two Cities*, Charles Dickens

2. *The Three Musketeers*, Alexandre Dumas *père*

3. *The Sign of Four*, Sir Arthur Conan Doyle

4. *Six Characters in Search of an Author*, Luigi Pirandello

5. *The Thirty-Nine Steps*, John Buchan

6. *Around the World in Eighty Days*, Jules Verne

7. *A Hundred Years of Solitude*, Gabriel García Márquez

8.   *The Hundred and One Dalmatians*, Dodie Smith

9.   *The Thousand and One Nights*, various

10.   *Nineteen Eighty-Four*, George Orwell

If you said *The Four Musketeers*, deduct a point – there is no book of that title. Admit it, you've seen the films, not read the book, and were just trying to be clever, weren't you?

5 Which Came First?

Cervantes (1547), Defoe (1660), Goethe (1749), Balzac (1799), Longfellow (1807), Brontë (1816), Whitman (1819), Hardy (1840), Wilde (1854), Chekhov (1860)

6 Which Came First 2: Some More Recent Ones

Forster (1879), Tolkien (1892), Fitzgerald (1896), Nabokov (1899), Orwell (1903), Sartre (1905), Beckett (1906), Bellow (1915), Solzhenitsyn (1918), Lessing (1919)

7 Natural Features

1B. an albatross, Coleridge, *The Rime of the Ancient Mariner*

2E. apes and peacocks, Masefield, 'Cargoes'

3J. daffodils, Wordsworth. The poem is called 'I Wandered Lonely as a Cloud', though many people refer to it as 'Daffodils'

4G. fields of barley and of rye, Tennyson, *The Lady of Shalott*

5I. leaves of grass, Whitman, *Leaves of Grass*

6D. a nightingale, most famously Keats, 'Ode to a Nightingale'

7F. a skylark, Shelley, 'To a Skylark'

8C. thistles, Hughes, 'Thistles'

9A. a tyger, Blake, 'The Tyger'

10H. willows and willowherb, Thomas, 'Adlestrop'

8 Potted Plots 1

1C IX. *The Grapes of Wrath*, Steinbeck

2D II. *Great Expectations*, Dickens

3I III. *Silas Marner*, Eliot

4F I. *Jane Eyre*, Charlotte Brontë

5E IV. *The Great Gatsby*, Fitzgerald

6B VIII. *Clarissa*, Richardson

7J VI. *Tess of the D'Urbervilles*, Hardy

8G X. *Kidnapped*, Stevenson

9H V. *Madame Bovary*, Flaubert

10A VII. *Buddenbrooks*, Mann

9 Potted Plots 2

1. *Don Quixote de la Mancha*, Miguel de Cervantes, 1605
2. *Tristram Shandy*, Laurence Sterne, 1760
3. *Northanger Abbey*, Jane Austen, 1818
4. *The Tenant of Wildfell Hall,* Anne Brontë, 1848
5. *Uncle Tom's Cabin,* Harriet Beecher Stowe, 1852. The cruel master, Simon Legree, is widely regarded as one of the most villainous characters in literature.
6. *A Tale of Two Cities,* Charles Dickens, 1859. The great sacrifice is that Sidney Carton goes to the guillotine in place of Charles Darnay, uttering the famous lines, 'It is a far, far better thing . . . '
7. *Crime and Punishment*, Fyodor Dostoyevsky, 1866
8. *The Jungle Book*, Rudyard Kipling, 1894
9. *Brave New World*, Aldous Huxley, 1932
10. *The Tin Drum*, Günter Grass, 1959. The toy is the tin drum of the title.

10 Where Did They All Come From?

1. *J. G. Ballard – China*, born 1930. Generally considered a British novelist, but his most famous work, *Empire of the Sun,* is based in his birthplace, the International Settlement in Shanghai.
2. *Saul Bellow – Canada*, born 1915. Closely associated with Chicago, where he moved at the age of nine, but born in Quebec.

3. *Albert Camus – Algeria*, born 1913. Moved to Paris while in his twenties, but set *La Peste* and *L'Étranger* in his homeland.

4. *Joseph Conrad – Ukraine*, born, to Polish parents, 1857 in what was then the Kiev Governorate in the Russian Empire. Settled in England in 1896.

5. *T. S. Eliot – USA*, born 1888. Moved to England in 1914 and became a naturalized British subject in 1927.

6. *Arthur Koestler – Hungary*, born 1905. Lived in Palestine and France before settling in England.

7. *Doris Lessing – Iran*, born 1919. Born to British parents in what was then Persia, where her father worked for a bank. Moved to Rhodesia (now Zimbabwe) when she was six and, because of her political campaigning and resistance to apartheid, is often associated with that country and with South Africa, although she came to Britain in 1949.

8. *Vladimir Nabokov – Russia*, born 1899. Moved to the United States in 1937 and wrote his most famous novel, *Lolita*, in English.

9. *George Orwell – India*, born 1903. His father was in the Indian Civil Service, but his mother moved him back to Britain when he was a small child.

10. *Saki (H. H. Munro) – Burma*, born 1870. This writer of quintessentially English short stories was the son of an Inspector-General for the Burmese, in the days when Burma (Myanmar) was still part of the British Empire.

11 Shakespeare Summaries

1. *Macbeth*
2. *Much Ado About Nothing*
3. *As You Like It*
4. *Henry IV Part I*
5. *Othello*
6. *King Lear*
7. *Richard II*
8. *A Midsummer Night's Dream*
9. *The Tempest*
10. *Twelfth Night*

12 Shakespearean Couples

1D III.   Duke of Albany, Goneril, *King Lear*

2A I.   Antipholus of Ephesus, Adriana, *A Comedy of Errors*

3H IV.   Bassanio, Portia, *The Merchant of Venice*

4C II.   Claudius, Gertrude, *Hamlet*

5E V.   Demetrius, Helena, *A Midsummer Night's Dream*

6B VI.   Iago, Emilia, *Othello*

7F X.   Leontes, Hermione, *A Winter's Tale*

8J VIII.   Orsino, Viola, *Twelfth Night*

9G VII.   Petruchio, Katharina, *The Taming of the Shrew*

10I IX.   Valentine, Silvia, *Two Gentlemen of Verona*

13 Shakespeare Locations

1I .   Illyria, *Twelfth Night*

2F.   Vienna, *Measure for Measure*

3E.   Navarre, *Love's Labour's Lost*

4J.   Sicily and Bohemia, *A Winter's Tale*

5G.   The sea and the island, *The Tempest*

6B.   England and then France, *Henry V*

7H.   Troy, *Troilus and Cressida*

8C.   Rome, Sardis and Philippi, *Julius Caesar*

9D.   Britain, *King Lear*

10A. Elsinore, *Hamlet*

14 Popular Misquotations

The correct versions are:

1.   *An ill-favoured thing, sir, but mine own:* from Shakespeare's *As You Like It*. The speaker is Touchstone, the jester; he's referring to Audrey, the woman he wishes to marry.

2.   *A prophet is not without honour, save in his own country and in his own house.* St Matthew's Gospel (chapter 13, verse lvii) is a bit more long-winded than the form we usually use.

3.   *I have nothing to offer but blood, toil, tears and sweat* is what Winston Churchill actually said, in a speech to the House of Commons in May 1940.

'Toil' presumably gets left out because it all sounds too much like hard work.

4. *The better part of valour is discretion* are Falstaff's words, in *Henry IV Part I*, meaning that too much courage becomes foolhardiness, which is a bad thing.

5. *'Excellent!' I cried. 'Elementary,' said he* is the nearest Sherlock Holmes gets to uttering the famous line. This is in the short story 'The Adventure of the Crooked Man', by Arthur Conan Doyle, of course, and first published in *The Strand* magazine in 1893.

6. *Heav'n has no rage, like love to hatred turn'd/Nor hell a fury, like a woman scorn'd.* It's from William Congreve's play *The Mourning Bride* (1697). The speaker is Zara, the 'woman scorn'd' herself, promising revenge on the man who has mistreated her.

7. This is the opening line of Shakespeare's *Richard III*, spoken by Richard himself. It isn't a misquotation as such, but if you quote these words on their own you alter the meaning completely. Add the second line and you get *Now is the winter of our discontent / Made glorious summer by this sun of York*. In other words, everything in the garden is rosy now that Edward IV (who is a son of the House of York) is on the throne. If you know the play you'll know that everything in the garden isn't in the slightest bit rosy, but that's another matter.

8. *Power tends to corrupt, and absolute power corrupts absolutely.* This is the guy I had never heard of – the historian and politician John Emerich Edward Dalberg-Acton, first Baron Acton. In 1887 he wrote these words in a letter to fellow historian Bishop Mandell Creighton. Just in case you didn't get the point, he followed it with 'Great men are almost always bad men.'

9. *There is no new thing under the sun.* A nit-picking one, perhaps, but this is the form used in the Authorized Version of the Bible (Ecclesiastes 1: ix). The New International Version says 'nothing', but it wasn't published until the 1970s, long after the misquotation had entered popular use.

10. *To gild refined gold, to paint the lily, to throw a perfume on the violet*: the speech, from Shakespeare's *King John*, goes on, describing all sorts of other unnecessary things to do. The speaker is the Earl of Salisbury, reflecting on the wastefulness of having a second coronation so that your supporters can pledge allegiance for a second time.

15 Other Playwrights

1C IX.   *Death of a Salesman*, Miller, 1949

2B I.   *Doctor Faustus*, Marlowe, 1592

3G II.   *The Duchess of Malfi*, Webster, 1623

4H V.   *An Ideal Husband*, Wilde, 1895

5D X.   *Look Back in Anger*, Osborne, 1956

6I VII.   *Our Town*, Wilder, 1938

7F IV.   *The Rivals*, Sheridan, 1775

8E VI.   *Saint Joan*, Shaw, 1923

9J VIII.   *A Streetcar Named Desire*, Williams, 1947

10A III.   *The Way of the World*, Congreve, 1700

16 Austen Marriages

1. *Pride and Prejudice*: Fitzwilliam Darcy marries Elizabeth Bennet; William Collins marries Charlotte Lucas; George Wickham belatedly marries Lydia Bennet and Charles Bingley marries Jane Bennet.

2. *Emma*; Frank Churchill marries Jane Fairfax; George – almost always known as Mr Knightley – marries Emma (Woodhouse) herself.

3. *Sense and Sensibility*: John and Fanny Dashwood are the brother and sister-in-law of Elinor Dashwood, who marries Edward Ferrars, and Marianne Dashwood, who marries Colonel Christopher Brandon.

4. *Persuasion*: Mary Musgrove, married to Charles Musgrove, is the younger sister of the heroine, Anne Elliot, who marries Captain Frederick Wentworth.

5. *Northanger Abbey*: James Morland, the heroine's brother, breaks off his engagement to Isabella Thorpe; Henry Tilney marries Catherine Morland.

6. *Mansfield Park*: Maria Bertram marries Mr Rushworth but later elopes with Henry Crawford; her brother Edmund Bertram marries Fanny Price.
   As to the number of Austen novels published during her lifetime, the surprise is that there are only four of them: *Sense and Sensibility* (1811), *Pride and Prejudice* (1813), *Mansfield Park* (1814) and *Emma* (1816). *Northanger Abbey*, sold to a publisher as early as 1803, was neglected by him and published posthumously, along with *Persuasion*. This was at the end of 1817, although the year 1818 is given on the title page.

17 Complete the Quotation

1H II 9. All in the *valley* of death rode the six hundred, 'The Charge of the Light Brigade', Tennyson

2I X 6. From the *waterfall* he named her, Minnehaha, Laughing Water, *The Song of Hiawatha*, Longfellow

3G III 5. If you can meet with *Triumph* and Disaster, 'If—', Kipling

4F IV 1. In England's green and pleasant *land*, 'Jerusalem', Blake

5J VII 8. Look on my *works*, ye mighty, and despair, 'Ozymandias', Shelley

6E VI 4. Much have I travelled in the realms of *gold*, 'On First Looking into Chapman's Homer', Keats

7D VIII 10. That is no *country* for old men, 'Sailing to Byzantium', Yeats

8C IX 2. There's some *corner* of a foreign field that is for ever England, 'The Soldier', Brooke

9A I 7. What passing-bells for these who die as *cattle*?, 'Anthem for Doomed Youth', Owen

10B V 3. Where Alph, the sacred river, ran through *caverns* measureless to man, 'Kubla Khan', Coleridge

18 And Again . . .

1G VIII 8. A *plague* o' both your houses!, *Romeo and Juliet*, Mercutio

2B II 3. For in that sleep of *death* what dreams may come, *Hamlet*, Hamlet

3F X 10. If *music* be the food of love, play on, *Twelfth Night*, Orsino

4E V 4. Love looks not with the eyes but with the *mind*, *A Midsummer Night's Dream*, Helena

5A IV 6. Is this a *dagger* which I see before me?, *Macbeth*, Macbeth

6J IX 9. O brave new *world*, that has such people in't, *The Tempest*, Miranda

7I I 2. The barge she sat in, like a burnish'd *throne*, *Antony and Cleopatra*, Enobarbus

8D III 7. The *evil* that men do lives after them, *Julius Caesar*, Mark Antony

9H VII 5. This blessed plot, this earth, this *realm* this England, *Richard II*, John of Gaunt

10C VI 1. What, my dear lady *Disdain*! Are you yet living?, *Much Ado About Nothing*, Benedick

HISTORY ANSWERS

1 Divorced, Beheaded, Died . . .

The queens in order are:

Catherine of Aragon	divorced
Anne Boleyn	beheaded
Jane Seymour	died
Anne of Cleves	divorced
Catherine Howard	beheaded
Catherine Parr	survived

In terms of survival, Catherine of Aragon is way out in front at 24 years. Then come:

Catherine Parr (3½ years, still going strong when Henry died);

Anne Boleyn (3 years);

Jane Seymour (just under 18 months);

Catherine Howard (16 months);

Anne of Cleves (6 months – he didn't take to her at all, but she too outlived him).

2 Which Came First?

Norman (1066–1154, William I–Stephen)

Plantagenet (1154–1399, Henry II–Richard II)

Lancaster (1399–1461, Henry IV–Henry VI, though you have to allow for a bit of coming and going at this point because of the Wars of the Roses)

York (1461–1485, Edward IV–Richard III)

Tudor (1485–1603, Henry VII–Elizabeth I)

Stuart (1603–1714, James I–Anne)

Hanover (1714–1901, George I–Victoria)

Saxe-Coburg-Gotha (1901–1917, Edward VII–George V)

Windsor (1917–present; George V–Elizabeth II)

George V changed the name of the royal house during the First World War because Saxe-Coburg-Gotha sounded too German (not surprisingly – it *is* German). He is thus the only monarch to have featured in two houses.

3 Which Came First II?

Theodore Roosevelt 1901

Wilson 1913

Mackenzie King 1921

Coolidge 1923

Franklin D. Roosevelt 1933

Eisenhower 1953

Kennedy 1961

Pearson 1963

Trudeau 1968

Reagan 1981

Note: US presidents are normally elected in November and inaugurated the following January. The dates given here are for the inaugurations, but you can still give yourself points if you said the previous year.

4 Let Battle Commence!

1066 Stamford Bridge: not really part of a war – this was the battle in which Harold of Wessex fought off a Norwegian invasion, before having to head south to face a Norman invasion at the Battle of Hastings; defeated, he lost both his life and his kingdom.

1415 Agincourt: a decisive English victory during the Hundred Years War (1338–1453) against France, a highlight of Shakespeare's *Henry V*.

1485 Bosworth Field: the final battle of the Wars of the Roses (1455–85) between the English Houses of York and Lancaster. It was here that Richard III was defeated by the man who went on to become Henry VII, the first Tudor monarch. According to Shakespeare, Richard, realizing that all was lost, cried out 'A horse! A horse! My kingdom for a horse!' at Bosworth.

1651 Worcester: the final battle of the English Civil War (1642–51), which resulted in a victory for the Parliamentarians. It was after this defeat that Charles II is said to have hidden in an oak tree.

1704 Blenheim: during the War of the Spanish Succession (1701–14), a famous victory for the British general John Churchill, who became first Duke of Marlborough. The war, as its names suggests, was fought over who would rule Spain and whether or not it would be merged with France to form a single kingdom. It wasn't.

1805 Trafalgar: the Napoleonic Wars (1803–15), between France and most of the rest of Europe. Trafalgar was the battle in which the British admiral Lord Nelson was killed, even as his ships triumphed over the French and Spanish fleet.

1815 Waterloo: the final battle of the Napoleonic Wars, a triumph for the British general the Duke of Wellington.

1915–16 Gallipoli: the First World War. A disastrous attempt by Allied forces – and most famously the body of Australian and New Zealand soldiers known as the ANZACs – to capture the Turkish capital Constantinople, knock Turkey out of the war and establish a safe sea route to Russia. Despite the courage and resolution of the ANZACs and other troops, the campaign was notoriously badly managed and under-equipped. The first day of the landings, 25 April, is still commemorated as ANZAC Day in Australia and New Zealand.

1916 The Somme: First World War. One of the bloodiest battles in history: it dragged on for four and a half months, by which time over 300,000 Allied soldiers had been killed or listed as missing.

1941 Siege of Tobruk: Second World War – a major victory for Erwin Rommel, the German commander known as the Desert Fox.

5 Where Will It All End?

Assassinated or deposed

Edward II: King of England, deposed 1327 and probably murdered later the same year.

Louis XVI: King of France, deposed 1791, executed 1793; this was the king who went to the guillotine during the French Revolution.

Spencer Perceval: shot and killed in the House of Commons, 1812 – the only British Prime Minister to be assassinated. The culprit was a bankrupt Liverpool broker seeking compensation from the government. There is no record that he received it.

James Garfield: assassinated 1881, having been US President for only four months. This time the killer was a disgruntled office-seeker.

Tsar Nicholas II: 'Emperor of All the Russias', forced to abdicate following the February Revolution of 1917; executed/murdered by Bolsheviks in 1918.

Indira Gandhi: Prime Minister of India, assassinated in 1984 by Sikh extremists in her bodyguard.

Died in office

Edward IV: something of a surprise, this one: Edward was King of England during the Wars of the Roses and spent a lot of his time on the battlefield. A prime candidate for violent death. But he died in his bed, of an unknown illness, in 1461.

Louis XIV: King of France, died in 1715 after reigning a remarkable 72 years – he was succeeded by his great-grandson because he had outlived the intervening generations. This Louis was the 'Sun King' who built Versailles.

William Pitt: British Prime Minister, died in 1806 at the age of only 46, possibly from alcoholism.

Warren Harding: US President, died unexpectedly, but after a period of ill health and in the middle of a gruelling media tour, in 1923. The conspiracy theorists are still out on this one, but he was certainly in office and almost certainly wasn't murdered.

Franklin D. Roosevelt: US President, died 1945, less than a month before the end of the Second World War in Europe (he had been President throughout). The cause was probably a stroke, but he had been unwell for some time.

Emperor Hirohito: Emperor of Japan throughout the Second World War and for many years before and after; he lost his status as a 'living god' following Japan's defeat in 1945. Died in 1989, at the age of 87.

6 Line of Succession

British monarchs

1D.   Stephen

2A.   Henry III

3C.   Richard II

4B.   Mary I

5F.   William IV

The red herring is William III.

American Presidents

1E.   Madison

2D.   Jackson

3A.   Buchanan

4B.   Cleveland (he is the only US president to have served two non-consecutive terms of office)

5C.   Hoover

The red herring is Taft.

7 Commonwealth Prime Ministers

1C. Sirimavo Bandaranaike, Ceylon/Sri Lanka

2B. Diefenbaker, Canada

3G. Lee Kuan Yew, Singapore

4A. Menzies, Australia

5F. Muldoon, New Zealand

6E. Nehru, India

7D. Nkrumah, Ghana

8I. Nyerere, Tanzania

9J. Obote, Uganda

10H. Verwoerd, South Africa (and yes, I know they are no longer in the Commonwealth, but they were then. In fact it was under Verwoerd's regime that South Africa left the Commonwealth.)

The chronology is tricky here, as many of them came to power at much the same time and several subsequently became president. Be lenient with your scoring system.

Menzies 1939: his first term lasted only two years, but he was in again from 1949 to 1966.

Nehru 1947: the first PM after Independence, served until 1964.

Diefenbaker 1957–63.

Nkrumah 1957, then President 1960–6.

Verwoerd 1958 until his assassination in 1966.

Lee Kuan Yew 1959. Remained in office until 1988, making him the world's longest serving PM.

Nyerere 1960 (chief minister). Became Premier in 1961 and was President 1962–85.

Bandaranaike 1960: the world's first female Prime Minister, went on to serve three terms totalling eighteen years.

Obote 1962, then President 1967–71 and again 1981–5.

Muldoon 1975–84.

8 A Royal Family Tree

1A. King John

1B. Edward I

2A. Mary I (Mary Tudor)

2B. Mary, Queen of Scots

9 Royal Spouses

1H. Anne of Denmark = James I, 1589

2J. Anne Neville = Richard III, 1472

3C. Caroline of Brunswick = George IV, 1795

4F. Eleanor of Aquitaine = Henry II, 1152

5B. Eleanor of Castile = Edward I, 1254

6G. Eleanor of Provence = Henry III, 1236

7A. Henrietta Maria = Charles I, 1625

8I. Marie Antoinette = Louis XVI, 1770

9E. Marie de' Medici = Henri IV, 1600

10D. Mary of Teck = George V, 1893

10 Because It Was There

1D. Cape Kidnappers, New Zealand, Cook

2H. Melbourne, Flinders

3G. Straits of Magellan, Magellan

4E. Yucatán Peninsula, Cortés

5B. Quebec, Champlain

6A. Northwest Passage, Amundsen

7F. Newfoundland, Ericson

8C. Bahamas, Columbus

9J. Calicut, da Gama

10I. Beijing, Marco Polo

11 Inventors and Inventions

In chronological order:

1C. Archimedes, an irrigation device known as the Archimedes Screw, 3rd century BC;

3E. Bacon, magnifying glass, thirteenth century;

7F. Gutenberg, movable type printing c. 1439

10H. Tull, seed drill, 1701;

6B. Franklin, bifocals, mid-eighteenth century

8I. Hargreaves, spinning Jenny, 1764

2A. Babbage, analytical engine, 1840s

4D. Edison, light bulb, 1870s

9J. Marconi, wireless telegraphy, 1880s

5G. Fleming, penicillin, 1928

12 What the Romans Did for Us

Roman: vending machine, concrete, fire engine, odometer, underfloor heating
Chinese: fireworks, paper, the oar, paper, playing cards

13 Renaissance Movers and Shakers

In order of date of birth:

9H. Petrarch 1304

1A. Brunelleschi 1377

8G. de' Medici 1449

5B. Erasmus 1466

7C. Machiavelli 1469

4I. Copernicus 1473

6E. Luther 1483

10J. Tyndale 1494

3F. Cellini 1500

2D. Calvin 1509

14 Column Inches

A3. Doric

B4. Gothic

C1. Composite

D6. Norman

E8. Roman

F2. Corinthian

G7. Palladian

H5. Ionic

15 Time Line of Unfortunate Events

1C. 1348, the Black Death

2K. 1533, Ivan the Terrible

3O. 1545, the *Mary Rose*

4N. 1634–8, the Pequot War

5B. 1642, the Battle of Edgehill

6I. 1666, the Great Fire of London

7M. 1755, the Lisbon earthquake

8H. 1845–51, the Great Famine

9E. 1861, the Battle of Fort Sumter

10J. 1883, Krakatoa

11D. 1899–1902, the Boer War (second South African War)

12F. 1912, Captain Scott

13G. 1916, the Easter Rising

14L. 1927, Stalin

15A. 1933, Hitler

16 But It Wasn't All Bad

1O. 1088, the University of Bologna

2I. 1215, Magna Carta

3M. 1471, Caxton's first book

4J. 1508, Michelangelo signs up for the Sistine Chapel

5K. c. 1590, Shakespeare's first play (opinions vary as to which it was – *Titus Andronicus, Two Gentlemen of Verona, The Taming of the Shrew* and *Henry VI Part I* are all contenders).

6G. 1605, Guy Fawkes

7H. 1687, Newton's Laws of Motion

8D. 1789, Bill of Rights

9E. 1796, Jenner's vaccination

10L. 1829, Stephenson's 'Rocket'

11A. 1856, Florence Nightingale

12C. 1876, Bell patents the telephone

13B. 1905, Einstein's Special Theory of Relativity

14N. 1918, women's suffrage

15F. 1953, Watson, Crick and DNA

GEOGRAPHY ANSWERS

1 Name That Town

1I. Abuja/Nigeria

2C. Banjul/Gambia

3B. Kinshasa/DRC

4G. Maputo/Mozambique

5J. Mogadishu/Somalia

6D. Nairobi/Kenya

7A. Ouagadougou/Burkina Faso

8F. Rabat/Morocco

9E. Tripoli/Libya

10H. Windhoek/Namibia

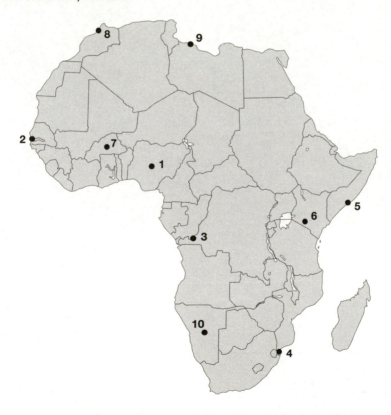

2 Name That Town 2

1F. Baghdad/Iraq

2J. Damascus/Syria

3B. Dhaka/Bangladesh

4E. Djakarta/Indonesia

5A. Kabul/Afghanistan

6I. Muscat/Oman

7C. Phnom Penh/Cambodia

8H. Pyongyang/North Korea

9D. Tbilisi/Georgia

10G. Ulan Bator/Mongolia

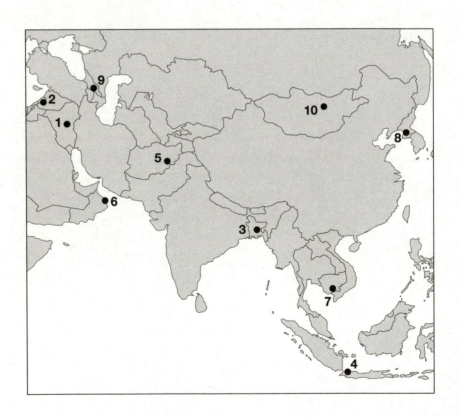

3 Name That Town 3

1I.   Belgrade/Serbia

2E.   Budapest/Hungary

3C.   Copenhagen/Denmark

4D.   Helsinki/Finland

5J.   Kiev/Ukraine

6H.   Lisbon/Portugal

7F.   Riga/Latvia

8A.   Sofia/Bulgaria

9G.   Warsaw/Poland

10B. Zagreb/Croatia

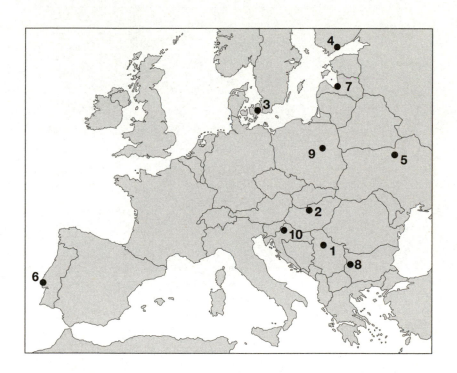

4 State Capitals

1F. Augusta/Maine

2E. Boise/Idaho

3J. Columbia/South Carolina

4I. Concord/New Hampshire

5B. Denver/Colorado

6C. Dover/Delaware

7G. Lansing/Michigan

8A. Montgomery/Alabama

9H. St Paul/Minnesota

10D. Tallahassee/Florida

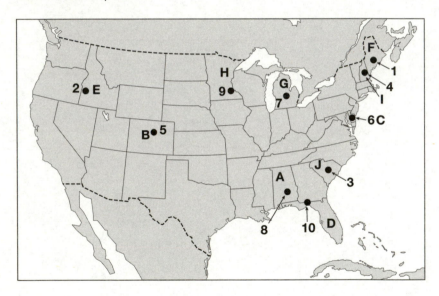

5 (Nick)name That State

1E. Bay State/Massachusetts

2I. Beehive State/Utah

3D. Bluegrass State/Kentucky

4C. Constitution State/Connecticut

5J. Evergreen State/Washington

6B. Golden State/California

7A. Grand Canyon State/Arizona

8F. Keystone State/Pennsylvania

9G. Mount Rushmore State/South Dakota

10H. Volunteer State/Tennessee

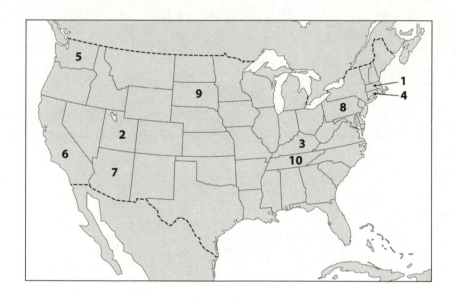

6 O Canada!

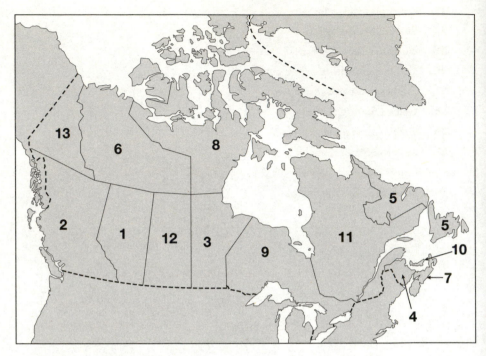

1. Alberta
2. British Columbia
3. Manitoba
4. New Brunswick
5. Newfoundland and Labrador
6. Northwest Territories
7. Nova Scotia
8. Nunavut
9. Ontario
10. Prince Edward Island
11. Quebec
12. Saskatchewan
13. Yukon

7 Australia Fair

1C. Australian Capital Territory/Canberra
2H. New South Wales/Sydney
3D. Northern Territory/Darwin
4B. Queensland/Brisbane
5A. South Australia/Adelaide
6E. Tasmania/Hobart
7F. Victoria/Melbourne
8G. Western Australia/Perth

8 Spoken Here

1C. Amharic/Ethiopia

2A. Arabic, French/Chad (they recognise this combination in Djibouti, too)

3I. Catalan, Galician/Spain (these are provincial languages spoken in specific parts of the country only)

4G. English, Tagalog/Philippines (in official contexts Tagalog is called Filipino, but it is to all intents and purposes the same thing)

5H. English, Tswana, Xhosa/South Africa. These are three of eleven official languages

6E. English, Urdu/Pakistan

7D. English, Yoruba/Nigeria

8J. French, German, Italian/Switzerland

9B. Greek, Turkish/Cyprus

10F. Spanish, Quechua, Aymara/Peru (they recognise this combination in Bolivia, too)

9 Climb Every Mountain . . .

In order of height:

Everest/Asia/8,848 metres

Aconagua/South America/6,960 metres

McKinley/North America/6,194 metres

Kilimanjaro/Africa/5,895 metres

Vinson Massif/Antarctica/4,897 metres

Blanc/Europe/4,811 metres

Wilhelm/Oceania (Papua New Guinea, to be precise)/4,508 metres

10 Ford Every Stream

Starting with the longest:

7. Nile (mostly in Egypt, but also in a number of other countries in north-eastern Africa) 6,670 km

1. Amazon (Brazil & much of northern South America) 6,450 km

9. Yangtze (China) 6,380 km

5. Mississippi-Missouri (USA) 6,020 km

10. Yenisey-Angara (Russia) 5,550 km

4. Mekong (Vietnam & Cambodia) 4,500 km

8. Paraná-Plate (Argentina & Uruguay) 4,500 km

3. Mackenzie (Canada) 4,240 km

6. Murray-Darling (Australia) 3,750 km

2. Danube (Germany & several countries in Eastern Europe) 2,860 km

11 Oceans, Seas and Lakes

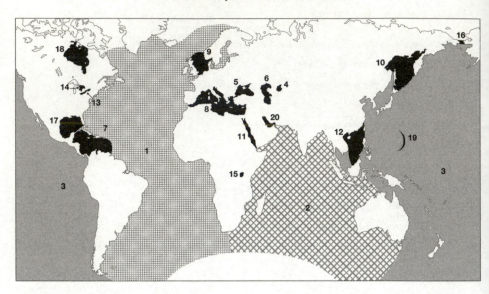

OCEANS

1. Atlantic
2. Indian
3. Pacific

SEAS

4. Aral
5. Black
6. Caspian
7. Caribbean
8. Mediterranean
9. North
10. Okhotsk (never heard of it? Shame on you! It's the sixth largest sea in the world.)
11. Red
12. South China

LAKES

13. Erie
14. Huron
15. Victoria

OTHERS

16. Bering Strait
17. Gulf of Mexico
18. Hudson Bay
19. Mariana Trench (at 11,022 metres, the deepest point in the world)
20. Persian Gulf

12 The Age of the Dinosaurs

1B. Ammonite/Devonian – up to 400 million years ago

2F. Coelophysis/Triassic – up to 250 million years ago

3D. Diplodocus/Jurassic – up to 200 million years ago

4E. Mammoth/Pliocene – up to 5 million years ago

5C. Sabre-toothed cat/Eocene – up to 42 million years ago

6A. Tyrannosaurus/Cretaceous – up to 145 million years ago

So, starting with the oldest, the order is Devonian, Triassic, Jurassic, Cretaceous, Eocene, Pliocene

13 Pick a Cloud

1D. Cirrus – thin wisps high in the sky

2A. Cumulonimbus – the stormy version of cumulus

3E. Cumulus – white fluffy clouds

4C. Nimbostratus – the stormy version of stratus

5B. Stratus – flat, greyish clouds that produce drizzle rather than heavy rain

14 Yes, Of Course I Know What That Is . . .

1. Lagoon

2. Caldera

3. Isthmus

4. Atoll

5. Monsoon

6. Mistral

7. Archipelago

8. Trade winds

9. Magma (when it reaches the surface it becomes lava)

10. Tsunami

MATHS ANSWERS

Where appropriate (and to stop some of the sums getting too scary) I have rounded answers to two or three 'significant figures', which saves me having to say 'approximately' every time.

NON-CALCULATOR

1 What's (or Where's) the Point?

A. $0.8 \times 0.4 = 0.1 \times 8 \times 0.1 \times 4 = (0.1 \times 0.1) \times (8 \times 4) = 0.01 \times 32 = 0.32$

B. $1.2 \times 0.04 = 12 \times 4 \times 0.001 = 48 \times 0.001 = 0.048$

C. $1.1 \times 1.1 \times 1.1 = 11 \times 11 \times 11 \times 0.001$

The easy way to multiply by 11 is to use the 'shift-and-add' technique: put a nought after the number you are multiplying and add it to the original number. So, let's assume you know your times tables and know that $11 \times 11 = 121$, you can then add $1210 + 121$ to get $11^3 = 1331$ so $1.1^3 = 1.331$

D.   Use last answer x 6 = 7.986

2 Scary Fractions

A.   143

B.   You'll find you can keep dividing them by 2 a lot, yielding:

$208 = 2^4 \times 13$

$352 = 2^5 \times 11$

C.   Recall that the lowest common multiple must have all the prime factors required to make each of the two numbers, so it's $2^5 \times 11 \times 13$. Using a lot of doubling (not too hard), you find that 2^5 is 32 and multiply that by part a) – I told you it would come in handy – to get 4576.

D.   To subtract one fraction from another, you need a common denominator, 4576, so multiply the tops accordingly:

$3/208 - 5/352 = (2 \times 11) \times 3/4576 - 13 \times 5/4576 = 66-65/4576 = 1/4576$

Phew.

3 Monty Hall

It seems as if you've got the same chance of winning either way. There are two doors left and the good prize is behind one of them. Fifty-fifty, surely? But it's not actually so.

It takes some thought. There is a $1/3$ chance that you picked the door with the prize originally, which means there is a $2/3$ chance that your first choice was coal. And because one of the pieces of coal has now been exposed, if your first choice was coal ($2/3$ chance, remember), then the remaining door *must* hide the prize. Changing your mind therefore doubles your chances of winning the prize.

4 Accent-u-ate the Negative

A. $-1 + 4 = 3$ (rewrite this as $+4 -1$ and it becomes obvious)

B. $3 - -2 = 5$ (two minuses cancel each other out and form a plus)

C. $6/-3 = -2$ (dividing a positive by a negative produces a negative)

D. $(-2 + 7)/-5 = -1$ (and again)

E. $3 \times (-2) + 14/-7 - 15/(-3 - 2) = -5$ (do the brackets first to produce $-6 + 14/-7 - 15/-5$; then do the division, remembering that dividing a positive by a negative leaves a negative. You now have $-6 - 2 + 3$. Rearrange it to put the positive first, $3 - 6 - 2 = -5$. Easy!)

5 At the Same Time

This being algebra, we need to use some letters, so let's call Constance's current age A, and Charlie's current age B (you wish they'd used different names don't you?). Decipher the question like this:

$A-3 = 2(B-3)$
$A+1 = B + 9$

Subtract the first equation from the second and you're away:

$4 = -B + 15$
$B = 11$

so $A = 19$

I hope Charlie is Constance's brother; otherwise she should really get some older friends.

6 Venn Diagram Fun

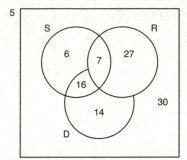

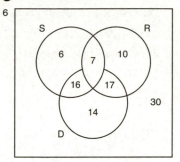

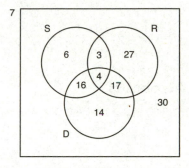

Armed with the information from 1 and 2, you can draw two overlapping circles, as shown on page 89. Put the number 29 in the S circle (29 people have snakes) and 34 in the R circle. The third piece of information tells you to put 7 in the area where the two circles overlap, as 7 people own both rabbits and snakes. You can then put 22 (29-7) in the S circle outside the overlap, as this is the number of people who have snakes but not rabbits; similarly put 27 (34-7) in the R circle.

Information 4 enables you to write 30 completely outside the circles: this is the number of people with no animals. When you add those with rabbits to those with snakes to those with no pets, and deduct the overlap between rabbits and snakes, you get 34 + 29 + 30 – 7 = 86, which leaves 14 people unaccounted for. These must be the people who have only dogs. Draw another circle, label it D, and write 14 in it.

Information 5 tells you that 30 people have dogs but no rabbits; you already know that 14 of them have only dogs, so 16 must have dogs and snakes. And so it goes on, adding more information to the circles at each step. Finally, in diagram 7, you come to the answer – 4, the number of the area where all three circles overlap (i.e. the number of people who have snakes, dogs and rabbits).

7 Get It Done by Friday

A. Do 3201 x 41 and multiply the answer by 1000

131,241,000

B. Slave away manually, or

(10,000 – 1)(100 – 1) = 1,000,000 – 10,000 – 100 +1 = 989901

C. 403:

```
        403
71) 28613
    284
     213
```

D. 101.21

8 Fraction Acrobatics

What you have to remember here is that dividing by x is the same as multiplying by $1/x$. So:

A. $7 \div 2 \, 1/3 = 7 \div 7/3 = 7 \times 3/7 = 3$

B. $1/2 - 1/3 = 3/6 - 2/6 = 1/6$. To divide this by a quarter you actually multiply it by 4, giving $4/6$ or $2/3$.

C. Start at the bottom of the sum: $1 \div 2 \, 1/3$ is the same as $1 \times 3/7$, which is $3/7$. So you now have to divide the 1 in the top line by $1 \, 3/7$ ($10/7$), which is the same as multiplying it by $7/10$ and, obviously, gives you an answer of $7/10$. Add that to 1 and the answer is $17/10$ or $1 \, 7/10$.

D. This is a 'lowest common denominator' problem. Convert all the fractions to sixteenths and you get $8/16 + 4/16 + 2/16 + 1/16 = 15/16$. Deduct the whole lot from 1 and you are left with $1/16$.

9 Hired or Fired?

Martha makes £150 on the first 50 jars. Then she sells 30 at 0.6 x £3 (remember, if we reduce the price by 40%, the new price is 60% of the original, i.e. 0.6 x £3).

30 x 0.6 x 3 = 18 x 3 = 54.

So her total sales figure is 150 + 54 = £204.

Her total profit is £204 – £95 = £109 so yes, she meets her target.

10 Mean, Median and Mode

Mean: this is what most of us call an average: the sum of heights (2087cm) divided by the number of youngsters involved (15), which to the nearest centimetre is 139cm.

Median: this is the middle number in the list, in this case the eighth: 140cm. If there was an even number of items in the list the median would be the midpoint of the middle two values. So knock the last one off our list to leave 14: the median is the difference between the seventh and the eighth (138 and 140), so 139. It is therefore possible for no individual height to be the same as the mean or the median. Weird but true.

Mode: the value that occurs most frequently, whether it is at the beginning, the middle or the end. In this case 145cm: the only one that crops up three times.

CALCULATOR

11 A Question of Scale

Pool: You can fit in eight times as much water, because multiplying lengths by 2 multiplies volumes by 2^3, which is 8.

Moon/Earth: Let E be the surface area of the earth, M the surface area of the moon and A the area of the blanket.

Then $E=3.67^2$ x M, because multiplying lengths by x multiplies areas by x2. To get a value for M in terms of E, we need to divide each side of that equation by 3.67^2, to give $M = {}^E/_{3.67^2}$.

$A = \frac{1}{3}$ x M as we've been told.

So $A = (\frac{1}{3}) \times \frac{E}{(3.67^2)} = 0.025$ E (or near enough for our purposes).

So the blanket only covers about a 40th of the earth's surface.

12 Sine Rule

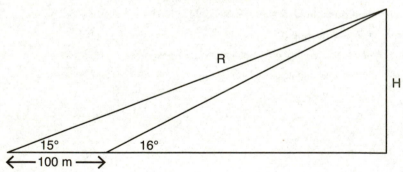

The sine rule states that $\frac{a}{sinA} = \frac{b}{sinB} = \frac{c}{sinC}$

So here $\frac{100}{sin(x)} = \frac{R}{sin(180 - 16)}$

x = 180 – 15 – (180 – 16) = 1 degree

$R = 100 \times \frac{sin(164)}{sin(1)} = 1579$m to the nearest metre

H = R x sin(15) = 409m to the nearest metre

13 How High the Cone

It'll help if you have that well-known trigonometric mnemonic SOHCAHTOA at your fingertips. This tells you that sine = opposite over hypotenuse, cos = adjacent over hypotenuse and tan = opposite over adjacent.

A.   6 sin(60) = 5.2 m to 2 s.f.

B.   2 x 6 cos(60) = 6 m

C.   recall volume of cone $V = \dfrac{\pi r^2 h}{3}$

use h from a), and r=3 (from b) to get 49m³.

14 Pythagoras

First we calculate the length of the diagonal, so we know how far Fenton has to run to express his rage fully. Using Pythagoras's theorem (the square on the hypotenuse equals the sum of the square on the other two sides), this is the square root of $50^2 + 75^2$, which, to the nearest metre, is 90m. Using time = distance/speed, we see that James has about 90 ÷ 8 = 11.3 seconds to get over that fence.

15 Declaring an Interest

A.   multiply 30 by 1.01 repeatedly until you get an answer of at least 31. You'll find that you want it to take me at least 4 days to pay you back.

B.   This is compound interest, where the amount of interest paid in year 1 goes into your capital and earns interest in year 2, and so on. To reach savings of £2377.97, Paolo has earned 3% interest for three years and 4% interest for two years, so we can calculate first that 3 years ago he had $\dfrac{2377.97}{1.03^3}$ = £2176.23 and 5 years ago he had $\dfrac{2176.23}{1.04^2}$ = £2012.

16 I Wish It Could Be Christmas Every Day

The company spends 400 x £4.70 making toys, a total of £1880.

The company gives away 100, leaving 300 to sell.

$\dfrac{3}{5}$ x 300 = 180 are sold at £12.

The remaining 120 are sold at £6.

So the company gets 180 x 12 + 120 x 6 = £2880 in sales.

The total profit is £1000.

17 All's Fair . . .

A. There are 4 possible outcomes, TT, TH, HT, HH, in 2 of which I get exactly one head, so the probability is $\frac{2}{4} = \frac{1}{2}$

B. After four tosses there are $2^4=16$ possible outcomes. 6 outcomes have exactly 2 tails:

TTHH HTTH

THTH HTHT

THHT HHTT

So our probability is $\frac{6}{16} = \frac{3}{8}$

C. I can get a 4 from: 1+3, 2+2 and 3+1, and there are 36 possible combinations of the 2 dice. So the probability is $\frac{3}{36} = \frac{1}{12}$

D. There are 216 possible outcomes (6x6x6) for the 3 dice. How can we get 4 as the score?

1+1+2

1+2+1

2+1+1

So our probability is $\frac{3}{216} = \frac{1}{72}$.

SCIENCE ANSWERS

Answers given in calculations are generally rounded to two or three 'significant figures', which saves me having to say 'approximately' every time.

BIOLOGY ANSWERS

1 Cell Reproduction

1. B
2. C
3. D
4. A

2 Gene Talk

1. A
2. D
3. E
4. B
5. C

3 Baby Blue-Eyes

50%.

Well, Sarah has brown eyes, so must have a brown allele. She must also have inherited a blue-eyed allele from her father (since blue is recessive, he must be homozygous blue to display the blue phenotype, so blue is the only colour he can pass on). This means that Sarah is heterozygous blue/brown. In order to have blue eyes, Michael must be homozygous blue like Sarah's father, so the child will definitely get a blue allele from him. Hence it's 50/50, all depending on whether the child inherits the blue or brown allele from Sarah.

4 The Flow of Blood

A.   Oxygenated blood is usually carried by arteries.

B.   Veins carry blood towards the heart, arteries carry blood from the heart.

C.   The aorta

D.   The pulmonary arteries, taking blood from the heart to the lungs.

E.   The pulmonary veins, taking blood from the lungs to the heart.

5 A Spoonful of Sugar

Insulin is a **hormone** produced in the **pancreas** which is used to control the level of **glucose** in the blood. When a high level of glucose is detected in the blood, **insulin** is released to lower the levels of glucose by promoting its conversion into **glycogen** by cells in the liver, muscle and fat tissue.

6 A Rose Is a Rose . . .

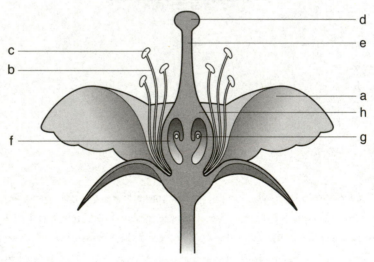

A.   Petal

B.   Filament

C.   Anther

D.   Stigma

E.   Style

F.   Ovary

G.   Ovule

H.   Carpel

7 Where the Heart Is

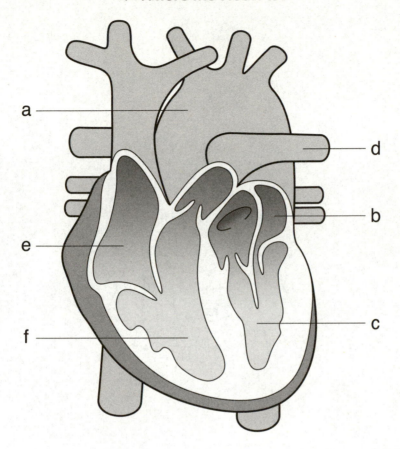

A.   Aorta
B.   Left atrium
C.   Left ventricle
D.   Pulmonary artery
E.   Right atrium
F.   Right ventricle

8 You Are What You Eat

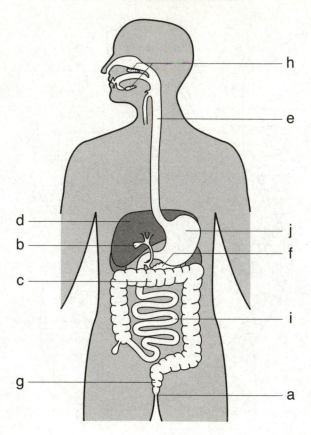

A. Anus
B. Gall bladder
C. Large intestine
D. Liver
E. Oesophagus
F. Pancreas
G. Rectum
H. Salivary glands
I. Small intestine
J. Stomach

9 The Air That We Breathe

Food + Oxygen = Energy + Carbon Dioxide + Water

There's also anaerobic respiration, the difference being that anaerobic respiration doesn't use oxygen in the process of releasing energy. A yeast colony can reproduce without the need for oxygen, for example, and a sprinter's muscles supplement normal aerobic respiration with anaerobic respiration to provide a burst of energy over those last few metres.

10 Fermentation

Glucose → Carbon Dioxide + Ethanol + Energy

11 Animal Cells vs Plant Cells

Plant cells contain chloroplasts, which conduct photosynthesis to make food from light, carbon dioxide and water. They have a fibrous cell wall made of cellulose.

Animal cells, on the other hand, are surrounded by a membrane through which certain substances can pass.

12 Starch, Sugar, Enzymes

To test for starch, add iodine solution. A dark colour indicates the presence of starch.
To test for reducing sugars, add Benedict's Solution and heat to 50 degrees Celsius for 5 minutes. A colour change to green, yellow or red indicates the presence of reducing sugars.

Water A	Solution in Visking A	Water B	Solution in Visking B
Neither	Starch	Reducing sugars	Reducing sugars and starch

Starch will very slowly break down in the absence of amylase (found in the saliva), but not quickly enough to show up here. The saliva helps the starch break down, and smaller sugars like glucose are able to pass through the Visking tubing and be detected in the water.

13 Plant in a Bubble

For the first three hours the plant is able to perform photosynthesis, absorbing carbon dioxide, storing food as a result and releasing oxygen back into the bag. For the next three hours, in the absence of light the plant uses this food to respire and produce carbon dioxide.

14 Immune System

'As part of our immune system we have two main groups of **white blood cells**, lymphocytes and phagocytes. **Phagocytes** are capable of ingesting or absorbing pathogens or toxins, and can also release an enzyme to destroy them. **Lymphocytes** on the other hand carry **antibodies** to bind to and render harmless an **antigen**.'

15 Eye of the Tiger

Eyes on front: likely predator
This configuration allows judgement of distances in a wide field, great for hunting down prey which is darting about in all directions and for assessing the best moment to pounce.

Eyes on side: likely prey
This gives 360° vision, allowing the animal to judge distances within a narrow field only. It's good for prey to see all around all the time, making it more difficult for a predator to avoid early detection.

CHEMISTRY ANSWERS

1 The Periodic Table

Alkali metals: potassium, caesium

Halogens: fluorine, iodine

Noble gases: neon, krypton

2 Atomic Bonds

Covalent bonds share electrons to complete orbits.

Ionic bonds exchange electrons to complete orbits.

Covalent: carbon dioxide, hydrogen, water

Ionic: potassium chloride, sodium fluoride

3 It's All a Balancing Act

A. $SnO_2 + 2H_2 \rightarrow Sn + 2H_2O$

B. $2NaOH + H_2SO_4 \rightarrow Na_2SO_4 + 2H_2O$

C. $CBr_4 + O_2 \rightarrow CO_2 + 2Br_2$

D. $6CO_2 + 6H_2O \rightarrow C_6H_{12}O_6 + 6O_2$

4 Some Hydrocarbons

1C. C_3H_6 is the unsaturated hydrocarbon with three carbon atoms per molecule.

2A. CH_4 is the simplest alkane.

3D. $C_5H_{10}O_4$ isn't a hydrocarbon.

4B. C_2H_4 is the monomer which forms polyethene (or polythene, or polyethylene or any one of a number of other similar names – they are all the same thing!)

5 Balloons

The order, from lowest to highest, is krypton, argon, neon, helium.

If balloons are of equal volume under the same room temperature and pressure, it means there are the same number of gas particles in each balloon – this is called Avogadro's Law, a name that I'm sure was in the back of your mind somewhere. So because krypton is the heaviest of the gases involved, the krypton balloon will be heaviest and can lift the least string before reaching equilibrium. Each balloon has equal up-thrust due to displacing the same volume of air, so it all comes down to their weights.

6 Ionic Compounds

Easier than it looks – you just need the same number of pluses and minuses

Compound	Constituent Ions	Chemical Formula
Sodium Nitrate	NO_3^-, Na^+	$NaNO_3$
Aluminium Sulphate	Al^{3+}, SO_4^{2-}	$Al_2(SO_4)_3$
Barium Bromide	Ba^{2+}, Br^-	$BaBr_2$

7 Testing Your Reactions

Alkali metals react more violently as you go down the periodic table, so:

A. Sodium
B. Potassium
C. Lithium

8 Name that Alkene!

In order, ethene, propene, butene; if we had more space we would continue with pentene and hexene as the number of carbons increased.

9 Fractional Distillation

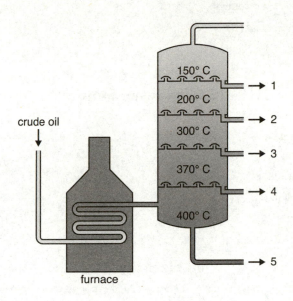

1C.   Gasoline

2D.   Kerosene

3A.   Diesel oil

4B.   Fuel oil

5E.   Lubricating oil, parrafin wax, asphalt

10 Cracking

Alkenes have some **double bonds** between **carbons**, meaning there is room for another **hydrogen**, or for linking to further **unsaturated carbons**.

Alkanes are hydrocarbons with only **single bonds**, whereas all **alkenes** have **double bonds** somewhere (otherwise they're not **alkenes**).

Alkenes can be used to make ethanol (alcohol) and polymers (plastics) due to the presence of these double bonds.

11 Sustainable Production of Alkenes

Aluminium oxide is a catalyst.

$$C_2H_5OH \xrightarrow{Al_2O_3} C_2H_4 + H_2O$$

12 Changes of State

1F. Sublimation

2C. Evaporation

3D. Freezing

4A. Condensation

5B. Deposition

6E. Melting

13 Electrolysis

Positively charged ions are cations. Negatively charged ions are anions.

In the diagram, A is the anode, it's positive and where the negative anions want to go. B is the cathode, it attracts the positive cations because it is negative. So the bromine gas forms at A and lead forms at B.

14 Ozone

$$CCl_3F \rightarrow CCl_2F + Cl$$
$$Cl + O_3 \rightarrow O_2 + ClO$$
$$ClO + O \rightarrow O_2 + Cl$$

15 Catalytic Converters

A) $2CO + O_2 \rightarrow 2CO_2$

B) $C_3H_8 + 5O_2 \rightarrow 3CO_2 + 4H_2O$

PHYSICS ANSWERS

1 Half-Life

$12.5 = 100 \div 8 = 100 \div 2^3$

So it will take 3 half-lives, i.e. 72,000 years.

2 Electromagnetic Spectrum

AM radio waves

Microwaves

Infra-red

Visible red light

Visible green light

Visible blue light

Ultraviolet light

X-rays

Gamma rays

3 The Line of Least Resistance

1. When S is open, no current flows – so 0A.

2. When S is closed, use Ohm's law V=IR with V=9 and R=8 to get $I = \frac{9}{8} = 1.125A$.

3. Use Ohm's again to yield 6.75V across the 6 ohm resistor and . . .

4. . . . 2.25V across the 2 ohm resistor.

4 A Tough One for Left-Handers

Using the right-hand rule, we see that the battery must have its terminals arranged like this:

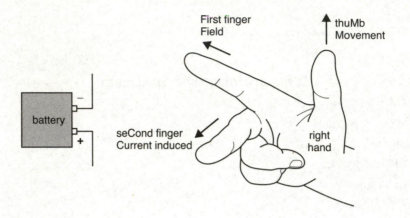

The right-hand rule works like this:

Your **F**orefinger points in the direction of the **F**ield.
Your se**C**ond finger points in the direction in which the **C**urrent is flowing.
Your thu**M**b points in the direction of **M**otion.

You point the two fingers you know (correctly assigned as above), and the remaining finger will point in the direction of the value you didn't know. So in our case we knew what to do with our **F**orefinger and thu**M**b because we know the direction of the **F**ield and that of the **M**otion. The result was that our se**C**ond finger revealed the direction of the **C**urrent. In other cases we might know the direction of current and field, and we'd be 'reading' our thumb instead to get the direction of motion.

So, in the diagram on page 125, look at the wire running horizontally nearest the S pole of the magnet (the lower half of the wire). Because of the way it's rotating (indicated by the arrow), that half of the wire is coming out of the page towards you, so your thumb should point towards you. Your forefinger points down to follow the direction of the magnetic field. That means (assuming you didn't mistakenly use your left hand) that your middle finger will be pointing to your right. So that's the way the current is travelling through the wire, left to right. Since, by convention, current travels from positive to negative, we assign + and

– as shown in the diagram on the previous page to correspond with the current going left to right along the bottom half of the wire. Note, if you'd done this while looking at the top half of the wire, it would be travelling away from you (so you would have pointed your thumb towards the page) and the current would go right to left (since it has turned around by that point). You'd get the same answer. And anyone watching what you just did is moving to a seat further down the bus.

5 Waves

v : wave speed

f : frequency

λ : wavelength

The note is $\dfrac{340}{0.25}$ = 1360 Hz

The wavelength of the microwave is $\dfrac{3 \times 10^8}{2{,}450 \times 10^6}$ = 0.12m, or 12 cm to the nearest centimetre.

6 Vanity

The normal from a point on a mirror is the line at right angles to the mirror through that point. Reflection always happens at equal angles to the normal. Recall that the angle of incidence/reflection is measured against the normal to the reflective surface. So both answers are 40 degrees.

7 Water Waves

The effect is called diffraction. Constructive interference occurs along A, B, C.

Sadly, because I'm trying to keep this relatively simple, I've had to reduce a complex concept to a pretty banal level here. But believe me, if you carry this idea forward into quantum physics, it can get very exciting indeed.

8 A Race Against Time

Distance travelled is the area under the graph. To calculate it, divide that area up into triangles and rectangles, by inserting three lines at right angles to the base up to points A, B and E. This gives, working from left to right, a triangle of 10 x 5, a rectangle 10 x 5, a triangle 10 x 3, a triangle 5 x 5 and a rectangle 4 x 5. Bearing in mind that the area of a triangle is $^1/_2$ height x base, we come up with this sum:

$$Area = \frac{(10 \times 5)}{2} + 10x5 + \frac{(3 \times 10)}{2} + \frac{(5 \times 5)}{2} + 4x5 = 122.5$$

So the motorbike travels 122.5m between O and F.

9 Hooke's Law

According to Hooke's Law, within its working range, a spring's extension x when at rest is proportional to the force applied. So if we double the mass (hence the weight, which in this case is the force applied), we double the extension. So x=2cm when we have 400g attached, and 2.5cm when 500g is attached.

10 Potential Energy and Efficiency

The lion weighs 250 x 9.8 = 2450N

So the potential energy gained by the lion during the lift is 6x2450 = 14700J

How much electrical energy did my pulley system use, though?

5000x8 = 40000J

$\frac{14700}{40000}$ = 0.3675, so my machine was only 36.75% efficient.

11 Expanding Universe

You should find that the frequency you hear is less than 440Hz, because the source of the wave is moving away from you. It's the same with stars: because the frequency you see is lower than that which you'd expect to be emitted at source, you see that the source is moving away from you. And that's why we say that the universe is expanding, because the vast majority of stars seem to be moving away.

OK? Are you with me? Then let's work out our problem. The peaks of the sound wave are emitted 440 times a second, i.e. once every $\frac{1}{440}$s. In $\frac{1}{440}$s, the car travels $\frac{20}{440}$ = near enough 0.045m. So the peaks arrive from the car to your ear every $\frac{1}{440} + \left(\frac{20}{440}\right) \over 340$ s. Taking the reciprocal to turn the time into frequency, you find the frequency you hear to be (to the nearest Hz) 416Hz. Which is, pleasingly, the 'bit under 440Hz' that you expected. Give yourself a bonus point.

12 Newton's Second Law

The law states that F=ma, force = mass x acceleration.
In our problem, let F be the forward force of the engine. The resultant forward force on the vehicle is F–150N.
Using Newton's second law, F–150 = 2000 x 2.
So F = 4150N.

13 Heat Transfer

A. Convection
B. Radiation
C. Conduction

14 Gas Laws

A. $8Nm^{-2}$

B. $\frac{4}{3}Nm^{-2}$

C. T = 450K, an increase of 150K

15 Gravity

Problems of this sort are often called 'suvat' because of the standard abbreviations they use:

s = distance

u = initial velocity

v = final velocity

a = acceleration

t = time

A. Use $v = u + at$, with u=0, a=3, t=2 to get $6ms^{-1}$

B. Use $s=ut+\frac{1}{2}at^2$ with u=0, s=6, a=9.8 and solve the quadratic to find t.
$6=4.9t^2$ so t=1.1s.

16 Drag Race

Use another of those equations, $v^2=u^2+2as$, with u=0, a=5, s=400.

V = 63.2ms.

17 Thirsty Work

Work done against friction = force x distance.

So I have done 60 x 20 = 1200J of work. And I think I deserve a beer.

18 Dogs and their Toys

Initially the ball is travelling away from him at 5ms⁻¹. The rate at which it is travelling away from him decreases at 0.5ms⁻², and it will be travelling towards him as soon as its speed drops below 10ms⁻¹. So we can use $u=5$, $a=-0.5$, and $s=-10$ to find t from:

$$s=ut+\frac{1}{2}at^2$$

$$-10=5t-\frac{1}{4}t^2$$

$$t^2-20t-40=0$$

$$(t-10)^2=140$$

$$t=10\pm\sqrt{140}$$

Taking the positive solution we see that $t=10+\sqrt{140}\approx21.8$s.

And at $t=10+\sqrt{140}$ the ball is travelling at $15-0.5\times t\approx4$ms⁻¹.

19 Specific Heat Capacity

Because SHC water is 4186 Jkg⁻¹K⁻¹ , we'll need $\frac{1000}{300}\times(100-15)-4186\approx1186033$ J to heat it. Because my kettle is 94% efficient, it will draw $\frac{1}{0.94}$ times this amount of energy to do the work. That's about 1261738J. At 3kW, this will take about 421s, so around 7 minutes and 1 second.

GENERAL STUDIES ANSWERS

1 Musical Instructions

1B.   Allegro – cheerful

2A.   Andante – at a walking pace

3H.   Cantabile – as if it were being sung

4D.   Diminuendo – growing quieter

5I.   Largo – slow

6J.   Pianissimo – very quiet

7G.   Presto – quick

8F.   Scherzo –playful

9C.   Staccato – detached

10E. Vivace – lively

2 Papal Bull

Bernardo.

There have been six Adrians (of whom the fourth was the only English Pope to date); five Celestines; one Conon; four Eugenes; at least three Felixes (five if you include two 'antipopes', which is too complicated an issue to discuss here); one Lando; five Martins; nine Stephens (a tenth, sometimes known as Stephen II, died three days after he was elected in the eighth century and no longer counts on official lists); three Sylvesters; and one Valentine. Eugene III's name before he became Pope was Bernardo of Pisa, but there has never been a Pope Bernardo.

3 Roman Numerals

1.   MLXVI

2.   MCDXV

3.   MDLXXXVIII

4.   MDCLXVI

5.   MDCCLXXVI

6.   MDCCCLXV

7.   MCMXLV

8.   MMI

4 Deus ex Machina

1E I.   Ceres/Demeter/crops and the harvest

2C IV.   Diana/Artemis/hunting

3G VI.   Juno/Hera/marriage

4J II.   Jupiter/Zeus/father of the gods

5B IX.   Mars/Ares/war

6G VII. Mercury/Hermes/messenger of the gods

7D X.   Minerva/Athena/wisdom

8I VIII. Neptune/Poseidon/the sea

9A V.   Venus/Aphrodite/love

10F III. Vulcan/Hephaestus/fire

5 The Muses

A tough one, this, because either you know or you don't. Give yourself extra points.

1D.   Calliope, epic or heroic poetry

2E.   Clio, history

3F.   Erato, love poetry

4G.   Euterpe, music and lyric poetry

5I.   Melpomene, tragedy

6H.   Polymnia, sacred song

7C.   Terpsichore, dance

8B.   Thalia, comedy

9A.   Urania, astronomy

6 Heroes and Heroines of Antiquity

1I. Achilles – the spot was his 'Achilles' heel'.

2B. Jason and his Argonauts found the golden fleece.

3F. Medea was not a woman to forgive and forget; the man who dumped her was Jason.

4C. Medusa had the snaky hair – she was eventually killed by Perseus, who used a mirror so that he wouldn't have to look at her.

5E. Oedipus was the one who ended up with the Oedipus complex. Funny that.

6J. All the evils of the world escaped from 'Pandora's box', leaving only hope behind.

7A. Paris ran off with Helen of Troy.

8G. Perseus rescued Andromeda not long after he had killed Medusa.

9H. Prometheus suffered this horrible fate. Mary Shelley's novel *Frankenstein* is subtitled 'The Modern Prometheus' because Frankenstein, in trying to create a human, was meddling in a domain in which mere mortals shouldn't meddle. Playing with fire, you might even say.

10D. Theseus killed the Minotaur with the help of Ariadne, who he promptly abandoned. There are not many faithful lovers in classical myth.

7 A Prophet in His Own Country

The major prophets: Isaiah, Jeremiah, Ezekiel

The minor prophets: Daniel, Hosea, Joel, Amos, Obadiah, Jonah, Micah, Nahum, Habakkuk, Zephaniah, Haggai, Zechariah, Malachi

The exception is the book known as the Lamentations of Jeremiah or just Lamentations

8 Biblical Quotations

1A. Am I my brother's *keeper?*

2E. Blessed are the *meek* for they shall inherit the earth

3D. Consider the *lilies* of the field, how they grow; they toil not, neither do they spin

4H. I am escaped with the *skin* of my teeth

5B. It is easier for a *camel* to go through the eye of a needle, than for a rich man to enter the kingdom of God

6I. Man is born unto trouble, as the *sparks* fly upward

7C. Suffer the little *children* to come unto me and forbid them not

8G. To every thing there is a *season* and a time to every purpose under the heaven

9J. *Vanity* of *vanities*, saith the Preacher, *vanity* of *vanities*, all is *vanity*

10F. Who can find a virtuous woman? For her price is far above *rubies*

9 The New Testament

1. Alexandrians

F. Timothy

Esther and Ruth

10 The Seven Deadly Sins

The sins are: anger, avarice, envy, gluttony, lechery, pride, sloth

The theological virtues: faith, hope, charity

The cardinal or natural virtues: justice, fortitude, prudence, temperance

11 Wonders Will Never Cease

Egypt: the Great Pyramid of Khufu (or Cheops), the Pharos of Alexandria

Greece: the Statue of Zeus at Olympia

Greek island: the Colossus of Rhodes

Turkey: the Mausoleum of Halicarnassus, the Temple of Artemis at Ephesus

Iraq: the Hanging Gardens of Babylon

12 Hindu Gods

1H. Krishna, the Supreme Being with the blue face

2D. Kali, the goddess of destruction

3E. Lakshmi, the goddess of light, beauty and good fortune

4A. Durga, the fierce warrior goddess

5B. Shiva, the destroyer with a trident

6F. Hanuman, the monkey-faced god

7G. Vishnu, the ever-wakeful preserver of creation

8C. Ganesh, the elephant-headed god

13 Composers

1C III. Antonín Dvořák, Czech

2I I. Arnold Schoenberg, Austrian

3D VIII. Edvard Grieg, Norwegian

4F VII. Franz Liszt, Hungarian

5B IX. Frédéric Chopin, Polish

6E II. Gustav Holst, British

7J IV. Jean Sibelius, Finnish

8A VI. Johannes Brahms, German

9H V. Maurice Ravel, French

10G X. Sergei Rachmaninoff, Russian

14 Musical notes

A. Crochet

B. Hemidemisemiquaver

C. Semibreve

D. Semiquaver

E. Breve

F. Demisemiquaver

G. Minim

H. Quaver

15 Musical forms

1J. Cantata, designed to be sung

2I. Chamber music, for a small group

3E. Concerto, a solo instrument backed by an orchestra

4D. Fugue, for a number of parts or voices

5C. Oratorio, a musical setting of a usually religious subject

6G. Prelude, usually designed to precede something else

7A. Rondo, in which a section recurs intermittently

8F. Sonata, for solo piano or piano and one other instrument

9B. Symphony, a large-scale work for full orchestra

10H. Toccata, played quickly and designed to show off the performer's skill

16 Great Artists, Great Works

1A. Botticelli, *The Birth of Venus*

2C. Constable, *The Haywain*

3G. Gauguin, *Two Tahitian Women*

4F. Van Gogh, *Starry Night*

5D. Manet, *Luncheon on the Grass* (better known as *Le déjeuner sur l'herbe*)

6B. Michelangelo, *David*

7J. Monet, *The Water Lilies*

8H. Rodin, *The Thinker*

9E. Velázquez, *The Maids of Honour* (*Las Meninas*)

10I. Leonardo, *The Virgin of the Rocks*

And the birth dates are:

Botticelli 1445

Leonardo 1452

Velázquez 1465

Michelangelo 1475

Constable 1776

Manet 1832

Rodin 12 November 1840

Monet 14 November 1840

Gauguin 1848

Van Gogh 1853

Give yourself lots of bonus points if you can put your hand on your heart and swear you knew that Rodin and Monet were born two days apart. And consider getting out more.

SELECT BIBLIOGRAPHY

Haines, Tim, *Walking with Dinosaurs* (BBC Books, 1999)

—, *Walking with Beasts* (BBC Books, 2001)

Kennedy, Michael, *The Oxford Dictionary of Music* (Oxford University Press, revised edition 1994)

Marriott, Emma, *I Used to Know That: History* (Michael O'Mara Books, 2010)

Marshall, Bruce, *The Real World* (Houghton Mifflin, 1991)

Osborne, Harold (ed.), *The Oxford Companion to Art* (Oxford University Press, 1970)

Ousby, Ian, *The Cambridge Guide to Literature in English* (Cambridge University Press, revised edition 1993)

Taggart, Caroline, *A Classical Education* (Michael O'Mara Books, 2009)

—, *Her Ladyship's Guide to the Queen's English* (National Trust, 2010)

—, *I Used to Know That* (Michael O'Mara Books, 2008)

— and Wines, J. A., *My Grammar and I (or should that be 'Me'?)* (Michael O'Mara Books, 2008)

Williams, Will, *I Used To Know That: Geography* (Michael O'Mara Books, 2010)

. . . and a great website:
www.cloudappreciationsociety.org